A PICTORIAL HISTORY OF
HENDRICKS COUNTY
INDIANA

NORTH SALEM STATE BANK

STATE BANK
of Lizton

LINCOLN FEDERAL SAVINGS BANK

A PICTORIAL HISTORY OF
HENDRICKS COUNTY
INDIANA

By

Linda Balough and Betty Bartley

THE
DONNING COMPANY
PUBLISHERS

Copyright © 1999 by Linda Balough and Betty
Bartley

For information write:
The Donning Company/Publishers
184 Business Park Drive, Suite 106
Virginia Beach, VA 23462

Steve Mull, General Manager
Ed Williams, Project Manager
Paula Ridge, Project Research Coordinator
Dawn V. Kofroth, Assistant General Manager
Sally Davis, Editor
Paul C. Gualdoni Jr., Graphic Designer
John Harrell, Imaging Artist
Teri S. Arnold, Director of Marketing

Library of Congress Cataloging-in-Publication Data

Balough, Linda, 1945–
          A pictorial history of Hendricks County, Indiana / by Linda
     Balough and Betty Bartley.
                    p.   cm.
          Includes bibliographical references (p.   ) and index.
          ISBN 1–57864–074–1 (hardcover : alk. paper)
          1. Hendricks County (Ind.)—History Pictorial works.   2. Hendricks
     County (Ind.)—History.   I. Bartley, Betty, 1950–   . II. Title.
     F532.H5B35   1999
     977.2'53—dc21   99–29868
                                                                   CIP

Printed in the United States of America.

Contents

Foreword

The Honorable Jeffrey V. Boles, Judge, Hendricks Circuit Court.

As WE GO THROUGH OUR LIVES, OUR families, school, and churches leave footprints in time. Our hopes, goals, successes, and failures are things that we must remember to guide us in the future. This *Pictorial History of Hendricks County* documents the growth of our county so that we can see and remember the past to help guide us in the future.

Industrial Souvenir of Hendricks County, State of Indiana

Preface

W. C. Newman was the proprietor of this early twentieth-century photographic studio. He specialized in the photography of groups and residences and was described as being active in Danville's social scene.

IN 1820 WHEN THE FIRST WHITE SETTLERS travelled into the area that would become Hendricks County there were no cameras to record the historic event.

It was not until 1839 that Louis-Jacques Daguerre created the daguerreotype that captured an image onto a silver-coated copper plate. It did not take long for the process, which originated in France, to appear in the County of Hendricks, State of Indiana.

By the time the first newspapers were printed in the county, advertisements for photographers or "Daguerrean Artists" appeared on their pages. Most of these early photographers traveled from one town to the next, recording the faces of those who wished to pay to have their images saved for posterity.

By the 1840s a few photographers made Hendricks County their permanent residence.

In the mid 1800s, the dry plate glass negative became available and made photography a popular amateur pursuit. When George Eastman invented roll film in 1888, a new era in photography began. The first "snapshot" cameras were made available to the public loaded with film and ready to use. When the roll was completed, the customer returned the camera to the company, where the film was developed, printed, and the camera reloaded with new film. "You push the button, and we do the rest" was the claim for the new Kodak cameras.

The twentieth century saw an increase in the use of photography by the public to record events in everyday life. Time brought advancements in technology, such as the capture of color and photos that developed instantly, free of the darkroom.

But despite all the changes from the early daguerreotype to today's digital imaging, the role of the photograph has remained the same: to capture an image, to record a moment, to create a piece of time that you can hold in your hand.

On the following pages are some of the images of Hendricks County's past moments, significant and insignificant, captured by the camera's lens and recorded, so this generation and those who follow can understand the people, whose lives are the text of our history.

As the reader sees the ebb and flow of the lives of those who have gone before us, frozen in time by the camera, it is our intention to show not only reflections of the past, but how those times mold the people, customs, and motivations of the present. Time and history are ongoing. Just as we look into the window of the past to examine our forefathers' lives, our lives are the history our descendants will study.

Through the production of this book, the importance of records of everyday living gained even larger significance. Letters long saved in ribboned bundles, journals, diaries, newspaper articles, even advertisements, and, of course, photographs, told us as much about how the earlier inhabitants of our county lived as did the historical documents. We have tried to find pictures which will tell about times of which the reader may not have memory or easy access. This is only a light touch on the intricate canvas of the history of Hendricks County.

We urge our readers to look deeper into the past. Read some of the books listed in the bibliography or other historical books about the county and the state. Examine collections of the past in museums and libraries. Become acquainted with the Hendricks County Historical Society. Perhaps readers will search their own shelves for pictures, letters, family and business records, and journals; and begin to study and record their own history so future generations can look back and see the people we are.

Acknowledgments

WE WISH TO THANK ALL THE PEOPLE who helped make this book possible:

The Hendricks County Historical Society
The Plainfield Public Library/Local and Indiana History Department
Guilford Township Historical Society
Danville Public Library
Avon/Washington Township Public Library
Coatesville Public Library
The Courthouse Grounds
C. M. Hobbs & Sons, Inc.
Hendricks County Commissioners
Margaret Hodson
Bob's One Hour Photo
May Loy
Timothy Balough
North Salem State Bank
State Bank of Lizton
Lincoln Federal Savings Bank

And to the countless other people who have encouraged and assisted with this publication.

Hendricks County Historical Society

1 The Birth of Hendricks County

The Northwest Territories

INDIANA'S FIRST WHITE EXPLORERS came, not from the east, or even from the south, via the Ohio River, the way many settlers would later enter the Indiana lands. The first traders came down the Ouabache River from the French territories in Canada. The Ouabache would eventually become known as the Wabash River and become an artery of commerce, eventually bringing families down into the southern end of its waters to establish a French-speaking town named Vincennes.

Port Vincennes was settled about 1702 and was hailed by travelers as a beautiful little settlement on the banks of the Wabash. The French government in the north encouraged traders to establish towns and forts all along the Mississippi and back up its tributaries to strengthen its claim to what they called the "Louisiana" lands, so other small settlements sprang up along the Wabash, Kaskaskia, and Illinois Rivers. The Spanish pushed their influence up the Mississippi, and the two converged at St. Louis. Later, Spain took control of the land west of the Mississippi and, at the close of the French and Indian War in 1763, the French ceded the land east of the Mississippi to Great Britain.

In 1778, George Rogers Clark captured Vincennes and turned the town's loyalties to American interests, specifically Virginia, which Clark represented. In 1783, Virginia gave the territory over to the Congress of the United States, and the Northwest Territory, which would become the states of Ohio, Michigan, Indiana, Illinois, and Wisconsin, was established, forbidding slavery and setting aside land to be designated for public schools.

Indiana Territory

Vincennes became the capital of the Indiana Territory with about fifty families living in the town including Territorial Governor, William Henry Harrison. The government began sorting out claims to land and establishing portions for sale.

The Indians were puzzled by the practices of the American settlers. One asked Harrison about this idea of possession of everything. "You call us children, why do you not make us as happy as our French fathers did? They never took from us our land, indeed they were common between us. They planted where they pleased; and cut wood where they pleased; and so did we. But now if a poor Indian attempts to take a piece of bark from a tree to cover him from the rain, up comes a white man and threatens to shoot him, claiming the tree is his own."

Statehood

In 1813, the territorial seat was moved to Corydon, on the Ohio River. On April 19, 1816, Congress established the State of Indiana and the first election resulted in Johathan Jennings being elected governor and William Hendricks as the new state's first Representative to the U.S. House of Representatives.

Immigrants flocked to Indiana. Some men who had fought in the War of 1812 had been given land in the territory as payment for their efforts and began claiming their land rights. Along with them came people from the East who had become disenchanted with the system of land distribution in states such as Virginia and North Carolina, where most of the land fell to the wealthy and others often only rented their farms from the landlord. In Indiana, land was for sale from the United States government.

In 1818, Governor Jennings negotiated the St. Mary's Treaty with the Indian tribes. The treaty stated the Indians would relinquish all the land south of the Wabash River, which included an area the Indians had used for a hunting ground which was to eventually become Hendricks County.

By 1820, some settlers had struggled through the deep woods of Hendricks County to establish little communities along the White Lick Creek and Eel River. They encountered plenty of wild game and rich

Hendricks County Historical Society

Above: The earliest settlers were attracted to the serene beauty of White Lick Creek and made their homes on its banks south of the present site of Plainfield. This scene, taken in the 1890s is of that same creek near Danville.

Left: The new land greeting the first settlers was abundant in game, fish, and some edible wild plants. Anyone who could fish or shoot shouldn't have to go hungry. Even by the middle 1800s, when this photo was taken by a well-known photographer J. P. Calvert, a person could expect a good catfish dinner anytime he had the time to throw in a line.

Hendricks County Historical Society

Logs furnished quick and easy construction material. Later, clapboard siding might be added, but most log cabins would be abandoned as soon as cut lumber and brick were available. This one, believed to have been in Clay Township, had been left to the weather for some time when this photo was taken around 1900.

Guilford Township Historical Society Collection/Plainfield Public Library

soil, but in order to build a home, the earliest settlers had to fell the oak, sycamore, beech, walnut, and poplar trees which grew in thick abundance all over the county. Once brought down, the oaks and poplars became the walls for the first houses and other trees the foundation for roadways, particularly through the swampy parts of the county.

Unlike the establishment of boundaries in the eastern states where border descriptions ran from "a boulder at the southeast corner, north along the stream bed thirty paces until met with a large oak tree overhanging the stream on the west bank, thence west for one hundred paces. . . ," Indiana was divided out in rectangular survey, with most counties having straight boundaries and ninety-degree corners. Within the counties, governed by a board of commissioners, came rectangularly shaped townships whose welfare was overseen by a township trustee and township school boards.

Hendricks County

After the signing of the St. Mary's Treaty, Hendricks County was the first county surveyed in 1819. On December 20, 1823, the Indiana General Assembly organized the County of Hendricks, effective on April 1, 1824, named for William Hendricks, then governor of the state.

The Townships

The county was first divided into ten, rather equal rectangular townships. Settlers rushed into the southernmost townships and soon had communities and then towns in Guilford, Washington, Liberty, then in Center, Eel River, and Marion Townships, but by 1840 only a scant few had populated marshy Union, Middle, Brown, and Lincoln Townships. Because most of that wetlands area was so challenging, the region was called the "black swamps" and was thought to be unhealthy.

The first settlers to arrive in Hendricks County came from Guilford County, North Carolina, many of them Quakers. They arrived in 1820 and named the township of their new home Guilford, after that of the old homeland over the Appalachian mountains, some seven hundred miles away. The town of Plainfield was settled primarily by Friends (Quakers), who connected with the first Monthly Meeting (the organizational unit of Friends) located just over the Morgan County line, in Mooresville. (For the first two years, Hendricks County was attached, for judicial reasons, to Morgan County.) Some of the first party to settle on White Lick Creek were Samuel Herriman, James Dunn, Bartholomew Ramsey, Harris Bray, John W. Bryant, George Moore, and his son Ezekial Moore.

Conditions were good for the settlers in this area and they were soon joined by others. In 1824, Guilford had more people than the rest of the townships combined. A trail to Terre Haute passed through the area, and people living along the trail not only had better access to markets and trading posts, but also could earn an income from providing hospitality to travelers and feed for the livestock that accompanied wagon trains or were herded along the trail to other markets.

Washington Township was one of the first four townships to be formed after the establishment of the county in 1823. The first settlement was near the present site of Shiloh Church. The community now known as Avon was first occupied in 1830, and has the distinction of having the most names of any town in the county. Hampton was its first name while Absolam Payne carried the mail by horseback. When he no longer wanted to carry the mail, delivery passed on to a doctor and then to another carrier, who tired of the duty and quit the job, so ending Hampton. In 1852, a new postmaster was selected for the town he named White Lick, but that endeavor only lasted for three months, and the name died. Later, a pack peddler, John Smoot, set up a store and named the place Smootsdell. He provided two mail deliveries a week. When the Indianapolis & St. Louis Railroad surveyed the line through the center portion of the township, a worker wrote "New Philadelphia" on a sign and stuck it in the ground. When the track was completed, someone from the railroad posted another sign with "Avon" on it and the name stuck. But it was not until November of 1995, in the wave of some of the fastest growth the county has seen, that Avon was incorporated as a town. It grew from a population of about 800 its first year, to 4,007 in December 1996.

Center Township was settled in 1823 and has, as its heart, the county seat of Danville, which was laid out in 1824 at the geo-graphical center of the county. Four men, Daniel Beals (Bales), George Matlock, Robert Wilson, and James Downard each provided twenty acres for the establishment of the town. On October 20, 1824, the county commissioners ordered fifteen gallons of whiskey to be available for refreshments and began a three day sale of the lots. Some lots went for as little as $3 dollars while, perhaps with the encouragement of the whiskey, others brought as much as $115.

When the subject for a name for the new county seat came up, a traveling judge, William Wick, suggested naming it for his brother, Dan, and the town became Danville.

Two years later, Danville had a population of two hundred people. Danville soon became known, not only as the center of county government, but also for the pure water from its wells. Its higher elevation than most of central Indiana was believed to produce a healthier water source.

Danville became not only the governmental hub of the county, but also one of the leading locations for culture and education. The courthouse and jail were built, businesses grew; churches and schools were established and in 1878 the town acquired a very successful college. Danville later boasted a large twenty-three-acre park, purchased in 1913, which is still one of the recreational centers of the county. It was renamed Ellis Park in 1972 for Harvey Ellis, a beloved, longtime park director.

The first white people to settle Liberty Township, were Thomas and William

Amo thrived with the popularity of the Vandalia Railroad which ran through the town.

Hinton. In 1829 William laid out Belleville, the third oldest town in the county. Belleville's location on the Terre Haute Trail (later the National Road) made it an important early day town. Cartersburg, laid out in 1850, and located along the Vandalia Railroad, had its early claim to fame with the construction of the Cartersburg Magnetic Springs Resort. Clayton followed in 1851, named for the Kentucky statesman, Henry Clay, and originally bore the name of Claysville, until it was discovered there was already a town of that name. In the southern portion of the township, Hazelwood and Center Valley were established and Hazelwood still remains, on the verge of being revived by being located near an exit of Interstate 70.

In Franklin Township, Judge Nathan Kirk set up a tavern and inn near the Terre Haute Trail, in 1820. Stilesville, laid out in 1828, but not incorporated until 1928, was named for an early settler, John Stiles, and acted as another stopping point for travelers on the National Road. In 1925, Stilesville suffered a devastating fire, but the townspeople soon rebuilt the destroyed strip of buildings on the north side of the National Road. It still serves the surrounding farming community.

While settlers came to the area in the early 1820s, Clay Township was actually carved much later from parts of Franklin and Marion Townships and was given the name of the highly respected presidential nominee Senator Henry Clay from

Above: Clayton's downtown area featured a line of the interurban in the middle of Kentucky Street in 1915.

Right: Early settler, John Martin, came to Hendricks County in 1856 at the age of twenty, while cohort, Oliver Wells arrived in 1833 when he was three. They seem to be planning some sort of mischief as they sit for the photo.

Guilford Township Historical Society Collection/Plainfield Public Library

Kentucky. The railroad was the "father" of the towns of Clay Township. Pecksburg, Amo, and Coatesville lay along the Vandalia Railroad, and thrived on the grain market and other commerce the railroad brought. Hadley and Reno were situated on another line, the Indiana and St. Louis, and after the decline of the railroads, the towns declined. The Coatesville tornado of 1948, nearly obliterated the towns of Coatesville and Hadley, but Coatesville was able to recover, though never as strongly as before. Amo, once hearty, is now a quiet, comfortable little village.

Marion Township made a late start of development, even though the Rockville Road, (for a time, known as the Pikes Peak Road) or U.S. 36, passed through it. When the settlers did begin to populate the area, they found the rich, glacial soil promoted fine crops and livestock. New Winchester and New Williamsburg were only five miles apart and platted at the same time in the early 1830s. The village of New Winchester survived and sported a high school as early as 1900, while New Williamsburg, or "Billtown" inexplicably faded away. Marion Township has been closely associated with Center Township in many ways, including fire protection and now, education—with a school merger with Danville and Center Township into the Danville Community School Corporation.

In the northwest corner of the county, Eel River Township first greeted settlers in 1824. The land is rich with streams feeding into the Eel River, and mills sprang up along the waterways. The first mill in the county was located along Rock Branch Creek. Unfortunately, none of the early water mills have survived.

Eel River Township's only platted town, North Salem, was laid out in 1835, and it enjoyed early success from traffic along the Ladoga Road and what travel there was on the streams and river. It is said that North Salem's prosperity got a real boost from the efforts of Jerry Page, who saw that a survey called for the Cincinnati, Hamilton, Dayton Rail Line to pass nearly a mile south of the town. He went to the railroad officials and convinced them they would save money by avoiding the ravines and rolling hills on the line they had planned and would find better ground by directing the railroad along an easier path—right through the town of North Salem.

It was a town of some conflicting social habits. There was strong religious sentiment, however, there was also a saloon, and a long standing still, operated in a cove east of town. Raucous behavior led to several separate killings in the area.

On the other hand, the population would often take their quiet leisure strolling or reading along a beautiful steam which sprang up from a failed attempt to drill a gas well. Other entertainment was enjoyed by gathering in a pleasant grove owned by James A. Hadley. The grassy portion offered a ready location for concerts of the many musical groups in North Salem, circuses, horse racing, and baseball.

Though not now a center for burgeoning growth, North Salem is building on its heritage, becoming a quaint mecca for antique shoppers.

Middle Township once covered a larger swath of the northern portion of the county until in 1851, when Union Township was cut out from the western edge of the township.

Wetlands and the "black swamps" covered most of the land area of both townships. In the portion that is Union Township, two towns rose up along the Crawfordsville and Indianapolis Road and the subsequent Indianapolis and Bloomington Railroad which paralleled it. Raintown (Rainstown)

has virtually disappeared. Lizton has survived, though an outbreak of cholera in 1873, devastated the town, killing twenty-four people in a three-week period. Two more towns, Montclair and Maplewood also penned their success to the railroad. They located along the B&O Lines further south of the Indianapolis and Bloomington Line. That proved successful until the popularity for rail passenger travel declined. Now, the two settlements are barely discernible from the rest of the countryside as the population moves out from Pittsboro and Indianapolis.

Hendricks County Historical Society

This photograph taken at Main and Maple, shows a typical day in downtown Pittsboro in the early 1900s.

Middle Township commerce and education centers around Pittsboro, located not only on the Crawfordsville-Indianapolis Road, (now U.S. 136) and the railroad, but now has access to Interstate 74. Pittsboro first held the name of Pittsburg (ironic, perhaps, since now the leading industry is a steel mill, which began operation in 1998 as Qualitec.) The name was changed to Pittsborough and finally to Pittsboro. Pittsboro became one of the most successful towns in the county. In the early 1900s when it was incorporated, the town boasted mills, grain elevators, the Olsen buggy and wagon factory, a hotel, and a number of professional and retail offices. After a bit of a slack period in recent times, Pittsboro is now enjoying a healthy resurgence.

In the northeastern portion of the county, Brown Township was settled in 1824, by James Brown. Growth was very slow in this region, and until recently remained a sparsely populated area. In 1863, the township was split into nearly equal parts, the northern part to remain Brown, and the southern part named for Abraham Lincoln. Brown Township has no towns and remains predominantly farmland, though now suburban growth from Indianapolis has brought more housing to the north-eastern corner of the township.

Lincoln Township is one of the smallest townships in the county, but is now faced with the same rampant growth as Washington Township to its south. The town that is now known as Brownsburg was platted by William Harris in 1834, and was originally known as Harrisburgh. Some of the population of this, and other townships in the northern section of the county, were Irishmen who were sent to construct the railroad through this part of the county in the middle 1800s and decided to stay. The Irish, having been familiar with methods to dry the marshy land of Ireland, were able to drain the former swampland of northern Hendricks County, making it viable for farming. The need for drainage led to the creation of the Lingeman Tile Works, where clay field tiles were made.

Once established, Brownsburg led a lively existence. Its proximity to Indianapolis made it an early stop for travelers on the way toward Crawfordsville and points west. One account cited by Peg Kennedy and Frankie Konvsek in their book, *Village of Brownsburg*, reported as many as one hundred Conestoga wagons around the Tavern Stand, at the corner of the Crawfordsville Indianapolis Road (Main Street) and State Road 267, (Green Street) where Harley's Restaurant is now. The presence of a number of Irish families also brought about the establishment in 1867 of St. Malachy Catholic Church as the first Catholic church in the county.

Suburban growth from thriving Indianapolis has reached Lincoln Township, making recent growth a predominately residential expansion. Access to Interstate 74 increases Brownsburg's appeal to workers who commute to Indianapolis and what was farmland in this township is quickly growing houses instead of corn or soybeans.

Hendricks County Historical Society

Tilden, in Lincoln Township
was one of the towns
which sprang up along
the route taken by the
railroad, and later virtually
disappeared. It was named
for Samuel Jones Tilden,
an unsuccessful presidential
candidate in 1876.

2 Landmark Government Buildings

Courthouse

HENDRICKS COUNTY WAS ORGAnized by an act of the Indiana Legislature on December 20, 1823, and became an official unit of government on April 1, 1824. The new county was named for the Indiana governor at that time, William Hendricks.

The land was surveyed using the Land System of the United States, which Congress had enacted on May 7, 1785. Under this rectangular system, the county was divided into ten townships, which were further divided into sections.

When it came time to select a site for the seat of county government, some suggested Hillsborough, the first platted town in the county to serve that purpose. The town was located about two miles east of the present town of Belleville, along the migration route that would become the National Road.

However, officials decided on a location at the geographic center of the county, where four sections of land joined. The owners of the land were Daniel Bales (or Beals), James Downard, George Matlock, and Robert Wilson. Mr. Bales and Mr. Downard each donated twenty acres "for the consideration of locating the county seat." Mr. Matlock sold his twenty acres to the county for one hundred dollars. Mr. Wilson sold the fourth section to the county agent for one thousand dollars.

On July 14, 1824, a stake was driven to mark the location of the courthouse near a point where the four sections of land joined. It was decided to name the new town "Danville," at the suggestion of visiting Judge William W. Wick, after his brother, Daniel.

The first courthouse was constructed of the native material at hand. The cost of the one-story hickory-log structure was $147. In 1831, the courthouse was made more refined by encasing it in brick. As the county grew, more room was needed for county records. In 1848, the commissioners approved the construction of another brick building south of the court house. This second structure held the offices of the clerk, auditor, and recorder.

In 1858, the commissioners made plans for a new, larger building to replace the two smaller ones. Isaac Hodgson, an Indianapolis architect, was selected to draw up the plans for a new courthouse.

William Miller and Company was awarded the contact for the new building, to be built at a cost of $38,744. The old buildings were removed and work began on the new, two-story brick and iron structure. In December of 1859, the contractor quit the job, and one of the county commissioners, Martin Gregg, was put in charge of finishing the project.

The courthouse was completed in 1862 at a cost of $62,000. The building featured two towers: a clock tower to the north, and an observation tower to the south. The business of the county was conducted in this courthouse until January 9, 1912.

An interior view of the brick courthouse in 1904 shows County Auditor D. D. Mills (right) and his assistants at work. The young man in the center used a special typewriting machine to make entries directly on the pages of a ledger saving the tedious work of hand-copying required in the previous century.

Industrial Souvenir of Hendricks County, State of Indiana

Left: Spectators gathered to witness the demolition of the old courthouse, which had suffered a roof collapse on a January night in 1912.

Right: Demolition of the courthouse building in 1912 revealed the thickness of the brick walls, which were constructed during the Civil War.

It was on that night the roof over the second-floor courtroom collapsed. Many attributed the collapse to a particularly heavy snow, but the commissioners had been advised months earlier that the roof supports were weakening.

None of the county records, stored in other parts of the building, were damaged when the roof fell in. Temporarily, the circuit court offices were moved into the Trotter Block on the southside of the square.

After inspection of the damage and deliberation by the County Council, it was decided to raze the structure and construct a new courthouse.

Debris was hauled away and the site slowly cleared, until only the square tower that had contained the clock remained. Standing taller that the tallest tree in town, the clock tower proved difficult to fell. Workers used dynamite in an attempt to collapse the structure, but only succeeded in damaging some plate glass windows in nearby businesses.

Finally, it was decided to remove bricks from the base of the tower and shore it up with timbers. What happened next was described in the January 11, 1912 issue of the Danville newspaper, *The Republican*:

"The timbers were fired a few minutes before twelve. It has been planned to have the tower fall to the southwest. A great crowd gathered at points of vantage about the square. There was much speculation as to the possible damage to business houses when the tower fell."

"But when the moment arrived, the immense structure fell 'in its tracks,' simply dropped as if the entire foundation had been removed. Only a cloud of dust and then only a pile of rubbish with the smoke pouring out of it."

Clarence Martindale was hired as architect for the new Hendricks County Courthouse and the P. H. McCormack Company of Columbus, Indiana as contractor. The cornerstone for the new building was laid on May 20, 1913. Along with new items, the contents of the cornerstone of the old courthouse were placed within the northeast corner of the structure.

The new courthouse was designed in the Renaissance style, and constructed with an exterior of Indiana limestone, with an interior featuring marble floors and wainscoting, with a stained glass skylight in the rotunda.

Most of the materials from the old brick courthouse were hauled away to fill in a ravine at the east end of Marion Street, but part of the bricks were used as the foundation of the heating plant for the new courthouse, constructed adjacent to the sheriff's residence and jail on South Washington Street.

The clock tower of the former courthouse stood tall among the ruins. The clock was removed and reinstalled in the new courthouse that was completed in 1915.

Hendricks County Historical Society

The cornerstone of the present courthouse was laid with great ceremony on May 20, 1913. A metal box was placed inside containing contemporary mementos. Also placed inside was a smaller tin box that had been removed from the cornerstone of the old brick courthouse which had been demolished.

Hendricks County Historical Society

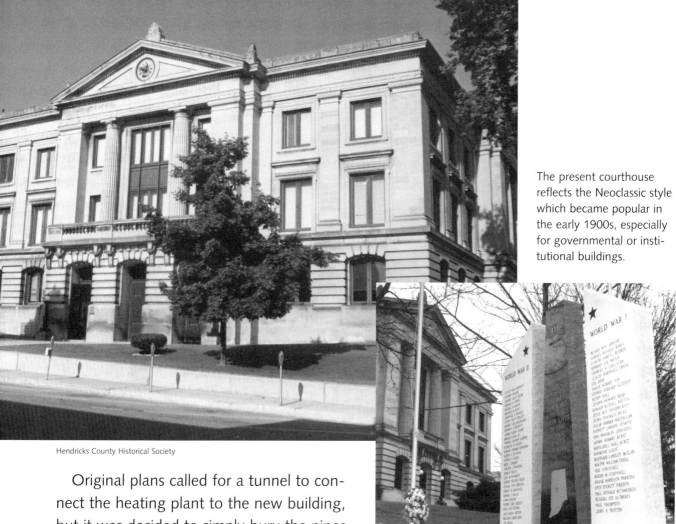

The present courthouse reflects the Neoclassic style which became popular in the early 1900s, especially for governmental or institutional buildings.

Hendricks County Historical Society

Hendricks County Historical Society

Original plans called for a tunnel to connect the heating plant to the new building, but it was decided to simply bury the pipes under the alley and street, and spend the funds on bronze doors and metal window frames in lieu of wooden ones.

After several years of digging up the alley to make repairs on the steam pipes, county workers constructed a tunnel to allow easier access for maintenance. Folklore has grown about the tunnel, with many people believing it was constructed for the purpose of transporting prisoners from the jail. Although it is possible the tunnel was used for that purpose on rare occasions, it was built for the use of maintenance men, not the sheriff.

A memorial to those Hendricks County soldiers who gave their lives during World War I and World War II, and the conflicts in Korea and Vietnam, was erected on the southeast corner of the courthouse grounds in 1992. The project was sponsored by the Danville and Pittsboro Jaycees.

Hendricks County Jail

Besides the Hendricks County Courthouse, another early structure built in most counties was a county jail.

The first Hendricks County Jail was built between 1830 and 1834. It was located on North Washington Street, about a half-block from the Courthouse Square. No photographs of the first jail have been located, but it was described as a two-story log structure, with an exterior stairway leading to the second floor. Below was a dungeon, or cell area. The only access was a trap door through which a ladder was extended and then removed when the prisoner was in place. The jail was surrounded by a high fence, also made of logs, which sometimes served as a holding pen for livestock confiscated by the sheriff or town marshal.

In 1838, the old jail was torn down, and a new log jail was built in its place, on the same site. The contract for the second log

The Hendricks County sheriff's residence and jail, completed in 1866, was the first building in the county in the Second Empire style of architecture. It featured a mansard roof and central tower. The men on the front steps are believed to be the sheriff and the county commissioners.

Hendricks County Historical Society

Hendricks County Historical Society

Thirty-two families occupied the sheriff's residence from 1866 to 1974. Jonathan S. Marshall, county sheriff from 1888 to 1890, posed on the front steps with family members and friends in 1889. This photograph was used in 1996, during the renovation of the building to recreate the missing columns on the porch.

jail stated the walls were to be two thickness' of square-hewn timbers, with a third thickness of timbers dropped endwise between them.

As sturdy as that sounded, the newspapers still recorded escapes. The September 19, 1857 issue of *The Butcher Knife*, one of the Danville newspapers, reported that four prisoners had escaped by prying a log in the ceiling aside and climbing into the loft. Once there, they broke through the gable end of the roof, and lowered themselves to the ground on a rope made from blankets and bed-ticking.

With the completion of the new Hendricks County Courthouse in the 1860s, the commissioners decided to have a new brick jail constructed, with a sheriff's residence attached.

Commissioner Martin Gregg, who supervised the completion of the courthouse

after contractors quit halfway through the construction, was chosen to design the new jail. He chose a new architectural style called "Second Empire," which featured a central tower and mansard roof.

The commissioners chose a location on South Washington Street and the building was completed in 1868. It was used by the county until 1974, when a new jail was built east of Danville, next to the County Home. The former jail and sheriff's residence was turned over to the Hendricks County Historical Society to serve as a museum of local history.

The structure still boasts the steel cellblocks with separate quarters for men and women. No visit to the county seat is quite complete without a chance to step inside the cellblock and hear the clank of the heavy doors closing upon the dark rooms. Prisoner art still adorns the walls. Simply viewing the old jail serves as an effective deterrent to misbehavior among visiting school children.

The sheriff's quarters are historically furnished and carefully maintained by the Historical Society with ever-changing displays of local history.

Hendricks County Historical Society

The Hendricks County Museum, located in the former sheriff's residence and jail since 1975, underwent an exterior renovation in 1997. The award-winning project included restoration of the columned porch at the main entrance and the contrasting patterned bands on the mansard roof.

County Home

The first County Home in Indiana, in Knox County, opened in 1824. Indiana Legislators put in place legislation to establish a county home in each county to provide a place for able-bodied people without a home to work, to support, and feed themselves. Soon, however, the county home, or county farm, also became the place for the elderly, the sick, and mentally ill and mentally handicapped. Often it was called the Poor Farm, Poor House, or the County Asylum.

Hendricks County's first county home was build on Twin Bridges Road, south of the present county home. Eldred Huff and Curtis King oversaw the construction of the building and, in September of 1838, presented a claim for $118.19 to the county commissioners for labor and materials for the property. The commissioner's records state:

> . . . the board being of opinion that said claim is extravagant and being disposed that right and justice be done between the County and the said superintendents do now appoint David Matlock and James Green to examine the said Poorhouse and estimate the value of work done and materials furnished. . . .

That order was canceled the next day, and Curtis King was allowed ninety-four dollars and six and three-quarters cents for materials furnished, and Eldred Huff was allowed one dollar for superintending. It is believed that building was brick. In 1846

Hendricks County Historical Society

another building was added to the acreage, this thought to be a frame house for the superintendent, while the brick was for the poor residents.

The current County Home, built in 1868, is one of only thirty left operating in the state. Each resident must be approved by the county commissioners. At one time, the residents worked at whatever jobs they were capable of doing to help maintain themselves. Some milked the cows, some cooked, some were able to help various ways with the farm chores.

The commissioners added more of the surrounding land to the county farm and acquired another farmhouse and farm buildings across the road for a farm manager. Now much of the county land houses the fairgrounds, the county extension agency and 4-H offices, the new county jail, the animal shelter, a building once used for an annex for county offices, the county garage, and the Hendricks Community Hospital.

Hendricks County Historical Society

Top: Since 1838, Hendricks County has provided a home for those without one. The present County Home is one of the few still serving that function in the state.

Bottom: At one time, the County Home sheltered not only the poor, but the insane. Several rooms in the basement of the building still have the barred doors used to keep inmates confined.

Hendricks County Government Center

The building now serving as the Hendricks County Government Center was built in 1928 as the Center Township School. The brick building at 355 South Washington Street in Danville once housed all the grades for the Center Township School District. After the old buildings from the former Central Normal/Canterbury College became available in the early 1950s for a high school, and a new North Elementary School was built on State Road 39, the Center Township School became South Elementary and served until the present South Elementary off Mackey Road was built. The old building on South Washington was abandoned as a school in 1994.

That year, Hendricks County commissioners J. D. Clampitt, Hursel Disney, and Richard Myers, saw the need to bring most

The Hendricks County Government Center is a fine example of wise rehabilitation of a historical building. This building, which once served all the grades of the Center Township Public School, became county government offices in 1994.

Photo by Linda Balough

of the county offices, which had been scattered in several buildings around Danville, under one roof and free up room in the courthouse for the sole use of the courts. An engineering study showed renovating the old schoolhouse would be less expensive than constructing a new building and would preserve a piece of Danville history.

The result was an award-winning renovation and new life for an old landmark.

Hendricks County Historical Society

3 Transportation

Bicycling became a popular means of transportation and recreation in the 1890s. "Wheelmen" like Orestes Hendricks, had their photographs taken alongside their "wheels." This sturdy model was needed for navigating the uneven roads of the county. Even so, he must have been highly challenged to ride this particular machine.

RIVERS PROVIDED THE FIRST ENTRANCE into the Northwest Territory, of which Indiana Territory was a part. While the terrain posed no mountains to climb, as had the Kentucky land to the south, Indiana was so densely covered with trees and brush, the first adventurers and trappers attempting to go inland could only follow narrow Indian trails. The earliest settlers traveled into Indiana along the Ohio River and up its tributaries and down along the Wabash from the French territories to the north, settling in towns such as Madison, Jeffersonville, and Falls of the Ohio, (later to be given the name of Louisville on the Kentucky side) on the Ohio River, Brookville on the Whitewater River near Cincinnati, and Lafayette, Terre Haute, and Vincennes on the Wabash River.

The National Road at the west edge of Plainfield was photographed by J. P. Calvert. The board fence at the lower right advises travelers to visit a local dry goods store for "cheap jeans and flanlins."

Guilford Township Historical Society Collection/Plainfield Public Library

In early Hendricks County, travel followed along the "Terre Haute Trail" located only a mile or so south of where the Cumberland Road, or National Road (now known as U.S. 40), eventually was carved across the country from Cumberland, Maryland to the Mississippi River.

When the settlers did blaze a trail through the woods, they often tied poles across the horns of their cattle as they drove them along the pathways. The trees were so dense the cattle couldn't get between the trees with the poles on their heads, so they had to stay on the road.

In the 1830s, the government began to see the value of inland travel to commerce, communication, and to unify the burgeoning country, and so began funding road construction. The work was done by the people who used the roads—often settlers would work on construction or maintenance in lieu of paying a road tax.

When the Cumberland Road was planned, the government building regula-

Van Buren Elm

Hendricks County was not blest with great navigable rivers, so the roads were the lifelines for supplies to come in and goods to go out to market.

When President Martin Van Buren failed to sign a bill to provide federal money to improve and maintain roads, the people of Hendricks County were not pleased. "The History of Hendricks County 1914–1976" edited by John R. McDowell, tells of an incident in Plainfield which brought fame to a venerable elm tree which stood in the yard of the Western Yearly Meeting on Main Street or then, the National Road.

Van Buren was campaigning through Indiana in 1842 in an attempt to be reelected after losing the presidential post in 1840. He traveled from Indianapolis to Terre Haute by mail coach and Phillip D. Jordan describes

Guilford Township Historical Society Collection/Plainfield Public Library

Left: The "Van Buren Elm" was the subject for a souvenir postcard.

Below: The Fisher Tavern at Plainfield, shown here circa 1910, briefly served as a presidential retreat when Martin Van Buren took a room while his muddy clothes were cleaned after the incident at the elm. The building later adopted the name "Van Buren Hotel."

Guilford Township Historical Society Collection/Plainfield Public Library

the ensuing "mud slinging" incident in his book "The National Road."

"A devilish plan took form. Van Buren would be taught what it was to toil along over a highway that jounced a man's liver sideways.

"Instead of walking his team the last half mile, Van Buren's driver [ed. note, a man from the Plainfield-owned coach company] lashed them to a frenzied gallop. As the presidential stage neared a treacherous mud hole, a favorite wallow for hogs, the driver yanked back on his left rein. The team reared and backed. The carriage slewed around to the left, its wheels cut under, climbed the bank and finally banged against the roots of a great tree. Slowly, very slowly, the stage overturned to land with a great splash in the center of the wallow. The agile driver jumped to safety."

The road was lined with people from all over the county who had heard Van Buren was coming. He climbed from the door uppermost on the coach and sloshed his way through the muck to Fisher's tavern where Mrs. Fisher helped to clean the mud off his pearl grey trousers, long frock coat, and wide brimmed hat. The 'plain' people of Plainfield had made their point.

A marker still stands on the spot honoring the huge "Van Buren Elm" tree, long since gone, which helped to dump an ex-president.

Illustration by Linda Balough

tions weren't especially exacting. Trees were to be cut, but stumps could be as much as a foot high in the cleared swath through the nearly always muddy path. Some accounts tell of pioneers trying to negotiate the roads which were often only passable three or four months of the year. The letters included descriptions of wagons buried to the axles in mud, wheels and axles broken by the projecting stumps.

Early road builders found the soft, sticking, black muck of the first trails unmanageable for travel by the narrow wheels of heavy wagons, so they logically took what was at hand to pave the road. They laid logs side by side across the roadway as a bumpy "corduroy road," then sometimes leveled sand or dirt over the top to smooth out the surface. After several years of lying covered with earth, many of the sycamore and poplar logs, which had been freshly laid after cutting, grew new trees at each end, forming a thick canopy over the lane.

(A portion of a corduroy road has been preserved along U.S. 421 in northern Indiana near Logansport. The ancient sycamores tower seventy-five feet toward the sky.)

"Gravel road" companies were formed by stockholders to build and maintain the roads and many routes were made toll roads, so those who used a road would pay for upkeep. Later "Plank road" companies paved the roads with thick wooden planks, but with the Hoosier winter freezes and thaws, the planks often heaved, creating even worse conditions than the mud ruts.

As commerce struggled on the roads, (the National Road was not paved through Hendricks County to Terre Haute until 1923) railroads emerged, which would be able to carry the loads of goods to markets all over the country. Hogs, cattle, turkeys, and chickens, could be transported by rail, as could cargo and people.

The first railroad through Hendricks was a line to connect Indianapolis to Terre Haute.

Train wrecks, such as this one near Amo in the 1890s were rare, but serious. On January 18, 1918, a freight train carrying ten cars of gasoline and five cars of crude oil derailed at the edge of Amo causing an evacuation and a fire which burned for several hours. There was no explosion and no injuries, but one woman who escaped the town reported that she did not run, but she passed several people who did.

Guilford Township Historical Society Collection/Plainfield Public Library

Completed in the 1850s, it ran through Guilford, Washington, Liberty and Clay Townships. Other lines soon followed and Indiana maps were crisscrossed with rail lines like so many veins. The railroad was indeed the lifeblood of many Hendricks County towns, which in the heyday of rail travel, thrived on the commerce brought by the roaring, powerful engines, puffing black smoke. Towns, affluent with lumber yards, grain mills and elevators, stockyards and factories sprang up along the tracks.

With the advent of the railroads, came some of the first commuters from Hendricks County to the State Capitol, Indianapolis. Ira Chase, governor of Indiana from 1891 to 1893 commuted from his home in Danville to the State House by train every day, since he didn't want to move his ailing wife to the capital city.

Commuting became even more common with the establishment of the Interurban System in the early 1900s. This electric train

A crowd gathered to greet the first interurban car in Plainfield in 1904. The interurban was a convenient (and clean) way to get from one town in Hendricks County to another and to the state capital, Indianapolis, while most of the roads were still dirt and gravel.

Guilford Township Historical Society Collection/Plainfield Public Library

A visitor's first impression was important, and the Danville railroad station strived to make that impression a pleasant one. The town's name was proudly and artistically displayed. To the right are the horse-drawn buses that would take the passengers to their chosen destinations.

Guilford Township Historical Society Collection/Plainfield Public Library

provided cheap and convenient transportation from the outlying areas around Indianapolis to the capital city. Hendricks county lines ran from Lizton, Pittsboro, and Brownsburg in the northern edge of the county; from the south from Amo, Cartersburg, and Plainfield; and centrally from Danville; into Indianapolis. (Plans existed to run the Danville line out to Rockville, but that never materialized.)

The convenience of the Interurban could not match the independence of another turn-of-the-century invention, the automobile. Indianapolis was a center for the production of the automobile, with names like Cole, Stutz, and Duesenberg. There was even one auto built in Hendricks County by wagon maker, Charles Olsen of Pittsboro. The buyer, James Hughes drove the sturdy machine for many years.

While by 1925, there were 2,485 miles of interurban tracks in the state, the automobile was gaining in popularity, and the

"electric streetcar" system was abandoned by the 1940s.

Pecksburg, North Belleville, Hadley, Tilden, Maplewood, Raintown (Rainstown), all once bustling towns along the tracks, have all but disappeared as the popular railroad and the interurban means of travel died out.

Before the railroads, the National Road had seen the swirling dust from thousands of settlers, and hundreds of thousands of hogs, cattle, and turkeys coming and going from the east to the western states of Missouri and beyond. People living along the road had become hotel keepers, tavern operators, and stock-feeding stations as the great migration followed the road to the west. As it, and other roads were improved and paved, the former Terre Haute Trail saw new businesses evolve from the old. Blacksmith shops became service shops for automobiles, dry goods, and general stores boasted gasoline pumps.

The Olsen was the only car built in Hendricks County. Charles J. Olsen was a Swedish immigrant who established a successful wagon factory at Pittsboro in 1882. He made only two automobiles—one purchased by James Hughes and the other by Jasper Swain. Hughes is shown in the driver's seat. His son, Ora, is on the left; son-in-law, Russell Brattain is the adult on the right. Grandson Ralph Hendrickson examines the car from the running board.

As automobiles became more numerous, so did the services offered by mechanical entrepreneurs. Scotten's Service Station in Stilesville, not only supplied gasoline and repairs, but a tow truck to retrieve stuck and broken-down vehicles.

Hendricks County Historical Society

Commuters who had abandoned the rails still liked the convenience of letting someone else drive and maintain a motor car, so bus services sprang up. In 1917, Danville boasted the first bus when the Pike's Peak Transfer was founded by H. Q. James. The August 20, 1951 edition of the *Danville Gazette*, describes the business through an interview with James. "Mr. James ran his bus from Rockville to Danville, one round trip each day." James brought Rockville passengers to Danville where they could board the interurban for Indianapolis, and returned them in the afternoon. James drove the gravel roads on solid rubber tires at a top speed of eighteen miles per hour (the fastest a four-cylinder International engine equipped with a governor would allow). His bus could carry seventeen paying customers besides himself, and the body

The Indianapolis-Rockville-Clinton bus schedule for 1928 was illustrated with a picture of the bus. The line ran through Hendricks County along what is now U.S. 36. The bus was frequently used by visitors to the tuberculosis sanitarium located near Rockville.

was hand made by "old man Olsen"—the builder of the only Hendricks County car and numerous school buses or hacks. James only operated that line for three months, and moved to operate between Rosedale and Terre Haute. But bus service revived in 1922. In the forties, Leighton Platter ran his nine buses from Danville to Indianapolis, some times on the half hour, sometimes every two hours, depending on the time of day.

As the prosperity of the "rail towns" fell off with the decline of the railways, the highway towns along the improved road system revitalized. A new kind of business emerged, as driving an automobile became something other than a way to get to market or to travel to conduct business. People found motoring in an automobile to be recreation—the "tourist trade" was born. The National Road became a major tourist thoroughfare and camping areas, rest stops with picnic tables, small diners, and eventually the "tourist house" with small sleeping cabins (the forerunner of the "motel") sprang up along the highway. Traveling by auto was an adventure.

Only after the Second World War, would President Dwight Eisenhower's wide-lane, fast Interstate highway system be able to draw drivers away from the charming drives along the two-lane arteries that had once again connected the lifeblood of the nation.

Even though the railroads lost their glamour as the highways and Interstates claimed travelers, and goods were transported by

The automobile heralded the growth of the tourist trade. This Plainfield "auto livery" featured "storage for tourists." To attract the attention of passersby, a signboard outside featured a clever quote: "Modesty, like the red plush album, has seen it's day."

Guilford Township Historical Society Collection/Plainfield Public Library

ever increasing numbers of semi trailers, much of heavy transportation is still done by rail. In 1959, the New York Central Electronic Freight Yard bought 526 acres in Washington township in Hendricks County and a portion of Marion County and built the Big Four Rail Yards. This facility is a sorting point for the railroad. It electronically scans and classifies the car numbers on a train. The cars are automatically sorted according to destination, directed to one of over sixty classification tracks and recoupled. The yard engines move the sorted lines of cars to the departure tracks where the big diesels haul them off to their destinations. The yard now works under the name of CSX Transportation, and an engine repair service has been added to the complex.

Hendricks County residents have enjoyed the sight of aircraft since the early days of man's flight, as residents with private planes and crop dusting businesses flew lower paths and giant commercial planes passed over from the airport just over the county line in Indianapolis. Now Indianapolis International Airport is beginning to have a larger impact on the county as it expands. Residents in the southern portion of the county near Plainfield can watch the lights and hear the roar of the engines as one of the busiest airports in the country at night sends its cargo planes into the skies. The arrival in the 1990s of Fed Ex and U.S. Postal Service parcel processing hubs, and the new United Airline maintenance facility have brought more residents to Hendricks County. As the airport expanded, Plainfield has become an ideal location for business, and companies have eagerly built in new commercial complexes just off the Plainfield exit of Interstate 70.

Transportation is still one of the major factors in Hendricks County's success, just as it has been since the first trees were felled to build the National Road across the nation.

Improved roads helped to link communities and businesses. Grading for drainage and packing the soil with steam rollers helped to keep roads more passable in bad weather. The crew constructing a road between Amo and Stilesville contained many local men who worked in lieu of paying county road tax.

Hendricks County Historical Society

Hendricks County Historical Society

Above: A handful of covered bridges once existed in Hendricks County. One was located on West Main Street in Brownsburg, which was part of the Crawfordsville-Indianapolis Road.

Top left: The importance of the horse as a means of transportation was reflected by the number of stables and liveries in business across the county. This is "Da" Burch's livery stables at Clayton, circa 1900.

Bottom left: Underage drivers were not prohibited from the roads in horse and buggy days. Young Kate and Mable Marsh could easily handle their two-wheeled buggy.

Guilford Township Historical Society Collection/Plainfield Public Library

Hendricks County Historical Society

Hendricks County Historical Society

Left: Wintry weather did not deter two gentlemen from Amo who hitched up their sleigh; a vehicle made to operate over slick and snowy roads.

Below: Snow removal was a group effort by the citizens of the Lincoln Township village of Tilden. Snow drifts often prevented residents of rural areas from traveling very far from home for several days or weeks.

Hendricks County Historical Society

Bridges of iron helped to span the county's many creeks and streams. A railroad bridge and a road bridge near Danville were nicknamed the "Twin Bridges." Although the railroad bridge was replaced with one of concrete, the nickname is still proudly used.

Hendricks County Historical Society

Without bridges, commerce would be severely hampered, so the construction of strong spans, such as this one near Cartersburg, were a high priority for county government. Only three examples of the fine iron bridges remain in the county today. One at a Washington Township park, one south of Plainfield and the smaller "twin" at Danville.

Guilford Township Historical Society Collection/Plainfield Public Library

Hendricks County Historical Society

Above: After a time, concrete construction was considered the preferred choice for bridges. A combination of man's muscle and machine was needed for the construction of this concrete bridge near Amo. After wooden forms were put together, wheelbarrows were used to fill them with the concrete mix.

Top right: An electric interurban car crosses a concrete bridge at Plainfield on its way to the "big city."

Bottom right: The interurban line ran down the middle of Indiana Street in Danville, then made a turn-around at the station. Passengers who wanted to go further west would have to hire a coach or take a bus ride.

Guilford Township Historical Society Collection/Plainfield Public Library

Hendricks County Historical Society

Guilford Township Historical Society Collection/Plainfield Public Library

The first automobile in
Clayton, about 1904–1905,
attracted an all-male crowd
of admirers.

Left: Some early automobiles closely resembled the horse-drawn vehicles they were replacing. Chester Phillips operated one of the early versions in Clay Township.

Below: W. L. Deweese and a passenger pose in front of Deweese's home in Plainfield. The conditions of the roads necessitated oversized front fenders to protect the occupants from splashing mud.

Hendricks County Historical Society

Guilford Township Historical Society Collection/Plainfield Public Library

Wilford Noel, Harris Weesner, and Lee Weesner used Harley-Davidson Motorcycles to carry the U.S. mail from the Clayton Post Office from 1912 to 1916. Motorcycles were not an uncommon conveyance for the unpaved roads of that era.

Guilford Township Historical Society Collection/Plainfield Public Library

Guilford Township Historical Society Collection/Plainfield Public Library

Above: Tourism was synonymous with adventure for early automobile enthusiasts such as Dr. Ernest Cooper of Plainfield. In 1913, along with his wife and daughters, he packed four hundred pounds of camping equipment in his new Ford touring car for a trip to Oklahoma. The loss of his leg was due to a hunting accident and did not deter his enthusiasm for the adventure.

Right: Bus service continued to be an important form of transportation in the county into the 1950s and 1960s. Pictured are drivers for the Danville Bus Line.

Hendricks County Historical Society

4 Home and Family

Home

James M. Barlow, born in 1845, grew up in this house in Washington Township and lived there during the early years of his marriage. After becoming an attorney and then a state senator, he moved up to several houses each grander than the last.

FOR THE EARLY SETTLERS, HOME WAS a place carved out of the wilderness. With the heavy tree cover over the county, the first shelter a family built on the newly acquired land was of logs—particularly poplar and oak. As romantic as a log house seems to be to us, the log cabins were only temporary in the eyes of the first settlers. Hendricks County residents wanted permanent frame or brick houses—they intended to stay and raise generations of children to continue to live on the farms and in the towns they cleared the land to build.

Many homes throughout the county were made of bricks fired on the site. Clay taken from the land under their feet was mixed with straw or other similar material and sand. The mixture was poured into forms, dried, and then fired in ovens near the construction. Most of the schools and

The basic needs of housing were met by the early log cabins, but they soon were cast aside for more substantial housing and buildings such as the ones most of the settlers had left back east. This cabin was razed to make way for a new Carnegie Library in Coatesville.

Guilford Township Historical Society Collection/Plainfield Public Library

churches were also built of "homemade" bricks until the coming of the railroad brought brick in from other parts of the country.

In both the country and town, "home" was a self-contained unit; consisting of the main house and a cluster of outbuildings: a carriage house housing the buggy or wagon and the harness horses, a smoke house to cure and store meats, a spring house for keeping foods cool—if you were lucky enough to have a spring on the place, a summer kitchen to keep the house from heating up in the hot, muggy days of summer, and a wash house for doing laundry.

Nearly every family cared for a small garden near the house to supply food and a few chickens to keep the bugs off the vegetables, provide a good supply of eggs,

Nearly every "home place" consisted of not only the family home, but various buildings, such as barns, outhouses, and spring houses. Sugar shacks like this one on John Milhouse's place were more rare.

Hendricks County Historical Society

Hendricks County Historical Society

Most farms and many homes with a bit of land near the towns were almost self-sufficient. Lois Shirley helps herself to a homemade pickle from the kitchen cabinet.

Guilford Township Historical Society Collection/Plainfield Public Library

These young ladies found a moment to pause near the family garden in about 1900. Notice the beans growing between the garden pickets behind them. The rail fences in Hendricks County were stacked five or six feet high to keep out roaming domestic animals not deer. *The History of Hendricks County, Indiana*, written in 1885, said the last deer in Hendricks County was seen twenty years before.

and Sunday dinner. The trees planted around the house earned their place by providing fruit to be canned or preserved for the winter. Likely a beehive would stand in the orchard to insure the trees and plants would produce, and to provide sweetening for homemade pies and cakes. If there was an arbor or perhaps a gazebo in a corner of the yard, chances are grapes would vine up the trellised sides, providing shade and food.

A "root cellar" often was dug over in one corner of the yard and covered with dirt and fastened with a sturdy door. Families would store potatoes, turnips, carrots, and winter apples, packed in straw,

Hendricks County Historical Society

The arrival of a new baby in the family was a joyous occasion for a visit from the photographer.

in the cool cellar, and run to it to hide if the Midwestern terror of a tornado came their way.

Life centered around the home. Babies were born at home, the sick were treated by a doctor who came to the house, and loved ones were "laid out" in the parlor when they passed away. Children were a part of the operation of the family, working along side their parents at plowing, feeding, haying, cooking, laundry, or whatever else had to be done. Many times they only went to school for the few months in winter when there were fewer chores and could be spared from the farm or business.

Hendricks County Historical Society

All too often the photographer would be called for a last, and sometimes only, photograph of the dear departed.

Leadership Hendricks County, Inc. saw the importance in knowledge of the past in understanding the present and in the development of the future. The members of Leadership Hendricks County chose the 175th anniversary year of the founding of Hendricks County to bring that history forth in a new manner with this Pictorial History of Hendricks County Indiana.

We, along with Lincoln Federal Savings Bank, North Salem State Bank, and State Bank of Lizton, the sponsors of this beautiful volume, are proud to have a part in the preservation of the history and memories of Hendricks County. The presentation of this pictorial account of our county's vibrant past gives us all a chance to reminisce about a time when struggle, triumph, strength and hope were essential parts of everyday life.

We hope this book will encourage interest and appreciation in Hendricks County's unique beginnings and reinforce the principles of family, community, faith, strength and honor on which the county was founded.

In the spirit of community awareness and family relationships, we dedicate this book to:

The citizens of Hendricks County Past, Present and Future.

Proceeds from the sale of this volume will benefit the programs of

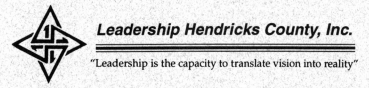

Guilford Township Historical Society Collection/Plainfield Public Library

William W. Quinn of Cartersburg, posed with son Harlan Evertt and grandsons, Lee and Harvey. Generations often stayed in the same area, often in the same house.

Families

Family was at the heart of the reasons for settling this area at all. While the Indians had very few permanent settlements in the area and used the land along White Lick and Eel River as a hunting ground, the white men came to stay. They settled in family and neighbor groups from other states, then often named the area for the place they left. Guilford Township and Pittsboro bear the names of places in North Carolina where some people left good homes and towns to buy land in the West where they could make their own destiny.

In-laws, parents, grown children, cousins, and uncles embarked on a mini-exodus to the new land, settled near one another and established bonds between themselves and the other settlers in a sense of close community that still exists across Hendricks County. It is often that "Community Feeling" that attracts many newcomers now, seeking what they instinctively long for: a sense of belonging and of the protection of knowing and trusting your neighbors.

Hendricks County Historical Society

One day in 1893, Ozella Furnas rode over to visit the Matthias and Matilda Hadley family in Amo. Others were there also. Elnora Hadley stands on the left next to Leora Harvey, next is Mr. and Mrs. Hadley as Loretta Hunt holds Ozella's horse. The Hadley boys perched along the fence are from the left; Orlando, Ozro, Orien, and Orvis.

Hendricks County Historical Society

Several generations are pictured at the home of John Hadley. Family reunions were an important way to link the generations together with traditions and oral history.

Reunions

Reunions became a means to renew the family ties as some of the children grew up and moved away. When better roads, railroads, and the call of lands further west lured some of the clan away, the reunion became a way to bring them all back together. Many families held annual gatherings which were all-day affairs.

Families gathered in a clearing near the old homestead. Very often the assemblage would be held in the family cemetery and children would play among the markers of their ancestors while adults reminisced about the times past. Tables were piled high with food, and entertainment was usually a "program" of a review of the family history, with recent updates, held just before the meal.

Hendricks County Historical Society

Family reunions became annual events in the early 1900s When descendants of John and Salome (Sally) Phillips had their reunion photographed in 1902, they included images of deceased family members, mounted on trees, in their portrait.

After the feast, children would play games or gather around under the trees and listen to the oral histories of the clan and county retold by the oldest family members as they sat in their favorite chairs brought along on the wagon from their parlors at home. Before leaving, the family would gather for a group picture. In many reunion photographs, there is a portrait of a deceased family member, or an empty chair to remind the group of "loved ones from our circle, gone."

Hendricks County Historical Society

Guilford Township Historical Society Collection/Plainfield Public Library

Hendricks County Historical Society

Top left: While many started out with simple homes, most aspired to ones like Roy Hodson's ornate mix of Italianate and other styles in Coatesville.

Top right: The Crawford House on U.S. 40 in Stilesville is typical of the simple lines of the Greek Revival style of architecture.

Left: Allen Whicker was born in a Clay Township log cabin in 1837. His later home, built in the same area, showed no nostalgia for his humble birthplace. The two-story mansion featured decorative features such as ornate metal railings, "gingerbread" trim, and a patterned slate. From his rocking chair on the front porch, the retired farmer could watch the newly planted trees grow to frame his new home.

Hendricks County Historical Society

Above: When newly married couples moved into a new home, they often marked the occasion with a photograph. Mr. and Mrs. Harry Hoadley posed proudly in front of their home near Maplewood.

Right: The "home portrait," a professional photograph of the house with the family members posed in front, was common in the late 1800s. Members of the John Franklin Keeney family brought out their houseplants and the family dog when the photographer came.

Hendricks County Historical Society

Guilford Township Historical Society Collection/Plainfield Public Library

Above: The family buggy was a source of pride as well as transportation. Cuthbert Osborn and his daughter, Ora, prepare to "go visiting."

Bottom left: Prosperous parents in the early 1900s displayed their offspring in ornate baby carriages. Young Nettie Owens was photographed at the home of her father, E. B. Owens, of Amo.

Bottom right: During the 1880s through the early 1900s, young boys under the age of six, wore dresses similar to those worn by girls. Many times their hair was left long until they enrolled in school.

Hendricks County Historical Society

Hendricks County Historical Society

Hendricks County Historical Society

Hendricks County Historical Society

Top: Friendships were highly valued by Hendricks County citizens. This group of young ladies had several portraits taken to commemorate their friendship.

Bottom: An evening's entertainment might include a friendly game of cards. Friends of the Huron family are pictured at their home near Danville.

Top: Besides the familiar large group portrait taken at family reunions, some smaller groups posed for the photographer as well. The sons and daughters of Eli and Peggy Phillips and John and Cathrine Cosner posed at a reunion held on William Cosner's farm near Stilesville.

Hendricks County Historical Society

Bottom: Relatives gathered for a photograph at the home of Benjamin Edmondson near Clayton. The house is one of several in the county to be placed on the National Register of Historic Places.

Guilford Township Historical Society Collection/Plainfield Public Library

By the 1890s, a nostalgia for the "old days" was prevalent. Aletha Coffin, mother of Addison Coffin, was posed at the Wilkinson studio at Danville with a spinning wheel, a symbol of the pioneer period. *The History of Hendricks County Indiana*, written in 1885, complained of the fast-paced lives and noted that some people longed for the days past when people had more time.

Hendricks County Historical Society

Hendricks County Historical Society

5 Community

District schools brought scattered rural families together to form a community. The school building was the site for exhibitions, recitals, "box socials," and other entertainments. Students at the West Lawn school held a special dinner on the last day of school.

ONE DID NOT MOVE TO HENDRICKS County without becoming part of the community. Those on the distant farms still found themselves interacting with their neighbors, at the district schools, at church, or at the various organizations, which sprang from the agricultural life, not to mention the teamwork among farmers at harvest time. The Farm Bureau, now a national farmer's organization, was founded by a Hendricks County group of hog farmers. The men banded together in December of 1918 as a voice to the Indianapolis Stockyards, which at a time of surplus pork supplies, had closed the gates to the hog raisers until their pens were cleared. The group negotiated with the stockyards officials, the marketing problem soon was solved, and a new farmer's organization was born.

Right: The North Branch Friends Meeting House was typical of the simplicity practiced by members of the Society of Friends, or Quakers.

Below: In the latter 1800s, the Society of Friends became influenced by Methodism, resulting in larger, ornate churches, such as the one constructed at Danville.

Guilford Township Historical Society Collection/Plainfield Public Library

Hendricks County Historical Society

Of course, churches created some of the strongest bonds between many people, of similar beliefs, and often, of similar heritage.

The first church in the county was the Regular Baptist Church, in what became Danville. At about the same time, Quakers, in what is now Guilford township, began attending their Meetings. (Quakers didn't consider their gatherings to be churches). Most of the religious groups in Hendricks County were Protestant or Quaker, until St. Malachy Catholic Church was established, in 1867, in Brownsburg, near a community of Irish, who had arrived in the 1840s. Several black churches were established in Hendricks County, such as the Bethel African Methodist Episcopal Church, on Vine and Lincoln in Plainfield, which had its beginning over one hundred years before as Black Rock Church, south of Plainfield.

Hendricks County residents were, and are, by and large, a group tolerant of differ-

Members of the African-American community played a role in the cultural life of the county. Bessie Siler and her twin sister, Hessie, played the guitar and gave poetry readings to clubs and churches.

ences. The settlers and the Delaware tribes, who were living on the banks of the White Lick Creek, peacefully coexisted until the Indians left, several years after the first white men set up homes; some records indicate the Indians even helped the new residents hunt and clear land.

While some covert slavery did exist in the early years, (though not openly called slavery, since a law, in 1787, prohibited slavery in any part of the Northwest Territories) black families, though not numerous, have figured as respected citizens, throughout the history of Hendricks County. Some of the early black settlers came with Quakers who might have purchased their freedom from slave masters back east. Others came alone as freemen.

The county participated in the underground railroad as slavery became more rigorously opposed, in the northern states, in the middle 1800s. At least three under-ground stations have been tentatively identified, in the county, in homes, or barns in Hadley, Lizton, and Danville.

By 1850, Hendricks County had a population of 14,083, of whom, forty-one were Negroes. A Negroes' Registry was kept at the courthouse listing physical description, occupation, place of birth, and residence. It seems to have been as much for the black persons' protection, as anything, so they could be identified as freemen and not runaway slaves. Black churches, social clubs, and literary clubs were established and several notable musicians and writers were black.

Black entrepreneurs ran barber shops; a Chinese family had a laundry in Danville, and early pack peddlers and hucksters were, very often, Jews who would look for a promising town, and then open a store, as did Joe Schwartz, who operated the Danville Department Store for many years.

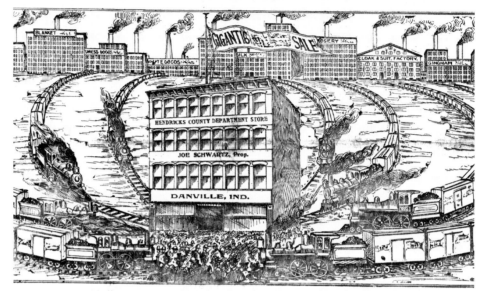

DANVILLE, IND.

reatest **DYER SALE** we have ever inaugurated
out for the **Yellow Tickets.**

| urkish Wash Rags, worth 5c Factory-End Price 2c | 1000 yards Colored Lawns, worth 6c, Factory-End Price 3¼c | 1000 yards of Dark and Light Challies, Factory-End Price 3¼c | Ladies' Hemstitched Hand-kerchiefs, Factory-End Price 3c | 1000 yards to 20 yds., F |

Hendricks County Historical Society

Joe Schwartz started out as a pack peddler and decided Danville was the place to establish his store. Starting with a small building in 1886, he was so successful, he built the building still standing on the east side of the square in 1897. When he died in 1902, his widow remarried and ran the store under the name of Schwartz until the 1940s.

The Civil War did divide some friends—and some families—and resentment persisted many years after the conflict had been concluded. Several groups of southern sympathizers worked against the efforts in the county to supply the Union with goods and food. There was at least one report of shots fired in a clash in Danville between a returned Union soldier and members of the Knights of the Golden Circle.

In recent years, the purchase of land by a Muslim group, known as the Islamic Society of North America, brought a new group of citizens to the county. This organization established its Muslim Student Association offices in Plainfield, and built a Mosque, on old Center Street Road, south of Plainfield near I-70. The group said they chose Plainfield, because of its central location in the country, (placing it within two hours of most of the Muslim population of the United States) and for its reputation of religious tolerance. The Islamic Center, an informational pamphlet, distributed by the organization, says, after evaluating more than ten cities in the Mid West, the society chose Plainfield because it found a higher educational level, broader social tolerance, lower crime rate, and a moderate cost of living. While there was some resistance to the group building on the 123-acre farm, it seemed to be primarily over fears the organization would conduct a mail order bookstore on the premises. The mosque and library, completed in 1983, now is an established addition to the landscape, and the people are accepted members of the schools and community.

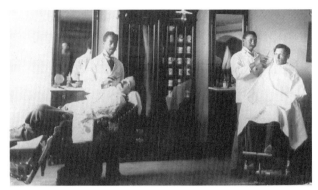

Hendricks County Historical Society

Guilford Township Historical Society Collection/Plainfield Public Library

As life in Hendricks County became more settled, more affluent people found time for more social functions. Men's organizations often met several nights a week. Masons, Odd Fellows, Red Men, Knights of Pythias, and Woodmen, were all fraternal groups, with initiation rites and secret handshakes. The Grange, as well as the Farm Bureau, was an association for farmers and growers, whose purpose was both social and business. The Grand Army of the Republic, made up of former Union soldiers, became very active in nearly all the Northern states, including Indiana. The G.A.R. held, as its purpose, to support Union veterans and honor the fallen of the Civil War.

Top left: John Foster (left) and John Moody operated the "2 Johns" barber shop in Danville. Barbering was one of the few trades open to African-Americans in the years after the Civil War. The personalized shaving mugs in the cabinet behind the men contain the names of prominent businessmen of the town.

Top right: The fellows loved to visit when they came to town for their Saturday haircut. This group is at Henry "Dutch" York's Barber Shop in Clayton in 1918. Dutch is at the back chair, Jim Coun is in the middle, and front chair barber is Glenn "Tige" York.

Hendricks County Historical Society

Fraternal organizations, such as the Lizton Knights of Pythias, were popular in the 1890s.

One secret society, the Ku Klux Klan, found a stronghold in Hendricks County from about 1915 through the 1920s. At one time, it was reported to have 2,457 members in the county. The group thought of itself as a benevolent patriotic organization, and listed as some of its philosophies, "Not for self, for others," and, in its constitution of Atlanta 1921, declared as its object—besides white supremacy—protection of the weak, innocent, and defenseless against the lawless and violent.

After the Civil War, there arose two organizations. One was the Horse Thief Detective Agency, a sort of quasi-legal vigilante group, whose aim was to locate and punish horse thieves and arsonists. The other was the Knights of the Golden Circle, who had been southern sympathizers. In a national resurgence of the Klan during the 1910s and 1920s, the KKK seemed to draw members from those two groups when strong sentiment in Hendricks County seemed to rise against Catholics. Several large gatherings assembled in the county during that era, one in Plainfield was said to number twenty thousand or so, but there was no violence ever reported.

One, the Klan was very strong all across Indiana during the time that D. C. Stephenson, the charismatic Grand Dragon, was in power, until his imprisonment, in 1925, for the murder of a young Irvington woman.

From an ad in *The Danville Gazette*

This gathering collected hundreds of Klansmen to Danville in 1923, the heyday of the Klan in Indiana before the murder trial of its Grand Dragon D. C. Stephenson.

The "social tea," held in the afternoon, became a ritual in many homes. Dainty foods were served, but the main purpose was the exchange of ideas, and perhaps a little gossip. Some unidentified young ladies used the "social tea" as a theme for a group portrait.

Hendricks County Historical Society

Women were not to be left out of clubs and intellectual pursuits. As nearly every household with even moderate income, by the middle 1800s, employed a "hired girl," who handled the laundry and household chores. Ladies found themselves with sufficient leisure time to shop, attend teas, volunteer their time to worthy causes, and to pursue cultural and intellectual activities.

Women figured in the establishment and operation of orphan's homes, a concept that seems to have not existed much before the Civil War.

They formed home economic groups, social clubs, and, of course, the women's organizations were often the backbone of the churches. The Women's Christian Temperance Union founded the Industrial School for Girls at Hadley. It was established in 1894, and operated for fifteen years, to house and train underprivileged girls as domestics or, hopefully, homemakers.

Across the country, the National Women's Suffrage Association influenced politics, while at the same time pressed lawmakers for women's rights to vote, to own and retain property after marriage, and to gain the right to custody of children after divorce.

Literary societies engaged both men and women, though rarely in the same organization. Members read, discussed, and wrote about the authors and philosophies, of the ancients, and of the current times.

The literary clubs in many Hendricks County towns often invited traveling orators to speak on the topics of the day. Chautauquas, band concerts, and traveling plays might grace any summer's evening or Saturday gathering, in a school, courthouse lawn, or park. Hardly a year went by after the Civil War, without a traveling stock company's presentation of "Uncle Tom's Cabin."

As Hendricks County residents today gather on the grass in Danville's Ellis Park, to

The following is an excerpt from "After 100 Years This Club Is Still Up To Date," by the author Linda Balough, an account of women's study groups, which appeared in the Metro West section of the *Indianapolis Star* October 16, 1998, upon the one hundredth anniversary of the Up-To-Date Club.

. . . According to Hendricks County Historian Betty Bartley, Women's study groups such as the Up-To-Date Club, which began in 1898 and is still active, had their beginnings when a newspaperwoman, Jane Cunningham Croly, wanted to hear Charles Dickens as he spoke at an 1868 New York Press Club meeting. The rules committee (which included her husband) refused to allow a "promiscuous" meeting. The term then meant having both men and women at the meeting.

"Mrs. Croly was unhappy. She was finally told if she could find 15 ladies who were willing to pay to attend, and sit together and entertain themselves, they could have a table. She told the Press Club, if they couldn't be treated as gentlemen, the ladies would not come."

That year, Croly founded a study club for women whose members would select a topic and present a paper on a selected subject at each meeting.

The idea became extremely popular, and in a few years Croly founded the Federation of Women's Clubs to unify the efforts and share their knowledge.

The first such club in Danville was the Browning Club, which is celebrating its 107th year. At that time Danville— a bustling community with its electric lights, brick paved streets, and well-respected Central Normal College could well accommodate several literary clubs and boasted many prominent members and guests.

The Up-To-Date Club was formed in 1898 with eight charter members, the oldest being Josephine Scearce Dungan at thirty-four.

Following the practice of their predecessors a century earlier, current membership is limited to a small enough number to gather at members homes.

"Uncle Tom's Cabin" was a perennially presented play in Hendricks County for many years after the Civil War.

COMING to Danville

Under a mammouth Waterproof Tent

HARMOUNT'S BIG

UNCLE TOM'S CABIN CO.

Friday, June 23

Show Grounds at the corner of Cross and Columbia Streets.

45 People
Band and Orchestra
10 Giant
Bloodhounds
2500
Comfortable Seats
Band Concert in the evening
All new, special scenery

Prices 25c-35c

Republican, June 22, 1916

Membership is by invitation to "women keenly interested in things current, cultural and educational," according to a history written in 1973 by member Margaret Baker. In the club's early days, even the husband was screened before a woman received an invitation.

Bartley confirms Baker's writing that the clubs filled a need for young married women who were intelligent and educated, but found the roles of wife and mother uninspiring.

According to Baker, each year's study papers have been printed and kept. In 1936, the year's program was placed in the cornerstone of the then-new post office.

Some of the early booklets contained as many as forty pages of presentations. They covered topics such as the 1899 presentations, "English Life and Thought" and "Childhood of the 19th Century." In March of 1900 the club examined the subject, "What Does the Opening of the 20th Century Reveal?"...

hear the summer concerts of the Indianapolis Symphony Orchestra, they are participating in a tradition started long ago by their forefathers. Nearly every town had a band. North Salem boasted a Boy's Band as early as 1894, and has held music in high regard for many years through groups such as the Ladies Choral Union and the North Salem Mandolin Orchestra. Schools of higher learning, such as Plainfield's Central Academy
and Danville's Central Normal College, had orchestras which performed often.

They may have started out in rough conditions in the wilderness of Indiana, but the residents of Hendricks County were determined to present as cultured an image

Guilford Township Historical Society Collection/Plainfield Public Library

School orchestras at Plainfield Academy and Central Normal College often gave concerts for the community. Academy schools offered music as a part of the curriculum, whereas the early district schools stuck to the three R's of read'n', 'ritin' and 'rithmetic.'

to outsiders, as that of any eastern city. Nearly every township started a library, as soon as it was possible after the county was established, and a "book wagon" made the rounds from Plainfield to the outlying farms as early as 1917. The county was able to attract four Carnegie libraries: Plainfield, located on Center Street just off East Main, now a residence; Brownsburg, on Main Street just east of State Road 267, now serving the Brownsburg Chamber of Commerce; Danville, at 101 S. Indiana Street, still being used as a library; and Coatesville, destroyed in the Coatesville Tornado in 1948.

Guilford Township Historical Society Collection/Plainfield Public Library

Hendricks County Historical Society

Above: The Plainfield Library's "auto-book-wagon" stopped at a farm home in Guilford Township. The vehicle was one of the first of its kind in the state.

Left: The Brownsburg Carnegie Library was built in 1916—the last Carnegie Library built in the county. Three of the four buildings are still standing, and Danville's, the only one to still be used as a library, has just undergone an expansion.

Right: The belfry was an important part of nineteenth century church architecture. The Methodist Episcopal Church at Danville featured an ornate tower to house the church bell.

Below: In 1856, the Western Yearly Meeting of the Friends was organized, and a brick building built in Plainfield. The Yearly Meeting covered the Quarterly Meetings of areas from Chicago to Mooresville. The new building couldn't hold all the attendees, so a women's group was separated and met separately until 1893, when the entire body was reconvened.

Hendricks County Historical Society

Industrial Souvenir of Hendricks County, State of Indiana

Industrial Souvenir of Hendricks County, State of Indiana

St. Malachy's Church in Brownsburg was the first Roman Catholic church in the county. The building shown was completed in 1904 and served about eighty families.

The family of John
Foster posed by their
house on South Kentucky
Street in Danville in 1894.
He was part of an African-
American community
that once flourished there,
and included two churches,
a fraternal lodge, and
a ladies' literary society.

Hendricks County Historical Society

Hendricks County Historical Society

Hendricks County Historical Society

Top: Former members of companies G and H, 99th Indiana Infantry met at a comrade's home in Danville. Regimental reunions became common after the Civil War. The friendships forged during that bloody conflict often lasted a lifetime. Many of the companies were made up of men nearly all from the same county.

Bottom: Some of the last Civil War veterans in Hendricks County posed for a group portrait circa 1934. Pictured left to right: William H. Nichols, Company B, 117th Indiana; John C. Russell, Company K, 70th Indiana; Thomas Coleman, Company H, 54th Indiana; J. S. Marshall, Company L, 21st Indiana Heavy Artillery; George W. Wood, Company A, 53rd Indiana; and James W. Beck, Company E, 33rd Indiana.

Although the men were
behind the pulpit, the
women were the power
behind the churches in the
county. The "ladies aid"
raised money for repairs
and redecorating with bake
sales and other fund raising
events. The women of the
Danville Methodist Church
posed in the building they
helped to maintain.

Left: While some women's clubs emphasized intellectual or charitable pursuits, some were organized purely for fun. The Jolly Belles of Clayton chose a comic pose for their portrait.

Below: Women's clubs provided social and intellectual stimulation for women of the late 1890s. The Browning Club at Danville was one of the first such groups in the county. Members are pictured at the home of Ora Adams, former president of Central Normal College.

Industrial Souvenir of Hendricks County, State of Indiana

The Thompson Eating Club seems to have attracted a large portion of the Danville residents at the beginning of the twentieth century.

Guilford Township Historical Society Collection/Plainfield Public Library

Left: Building character was the purpose of the Boy Scouts of America, founded in 1910. The troop at Pittsboro, shown here, was organized in 1924.

Below: The spectacle of a parade is enjoyed by young and old alike, no matter what the occasion. A political parade at Danville, circa 1900, gathered a large crowd.

Hendricks County Historical Society

Guilford Township Historical Society Collection/Plainfield Public Library

Left: Pride in the past has been a way of life in Hendricks County. During the Brownsburg Centennial in 1945, a commemorative photo was published showing growth of business on the main street.

Below: A modern interpretation of pioneer life was part of the celebration of Brownsburg's Centennial.

Hendricks County Historical Society

6 Confronting Crisis

WHILE EVERY COMMUNITY SOMEtimes faces the wrath of nature, or the worst of man, Hendricks County has been generally blessed with good fortune. However, some events stand out in history, which brought great tragedy to the residents of the county.

The Ill-fated Wagon Train

In 1849, a group of people set out from Ohio hoping to make a new life in California. They loaded up a wagon train of huge Conestoga wagons, pulled by oxen, the best animal to make the difficult trip. Each day was slow going over the National Road, and they made camp along the way, buying food from the farmers along the road for each night's meal, to lessen the provisions they would have to carry. When the group settled in for the night near Stilesville, they brought out their

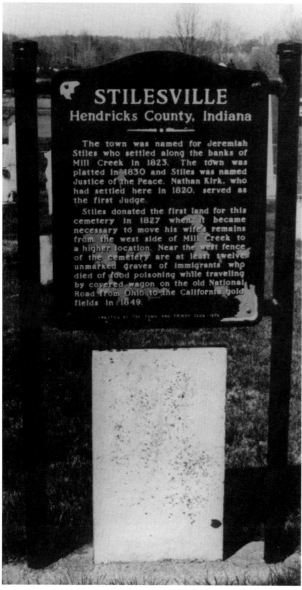

A marker posted by the town and Friday Club in 1970 at the Stilesville Cemetery remembers the victims of the ill-fated wagon train of gold-seeking forty-niners on their way to California.

William Shirley, of Clayton, was one of several officers that served from the county during the Civil War.

Guilford Township Historical Society Collection/Plainfield Public Library

Hendricks County Historical Society

pots; everyone pitched in for the shared meal, and someone prepared new corn, cooked in a copper kettle. The next morning they passed around the left-over corn, which had been sitting in the copper kettle over night. People immediately began falling ill from food poisoning. Estimates are that townspeople buried nineteen strangers from the wagon train, in the little cemetery in nearby Stilesville, in unmarked graves. The trail west, for them, was over.

Civil War

The Civil War broke out on April 12, 1861, when Hendricks County had a population of seventeen thousand. At Lincoln's call for fighting men, two thousand or 65 percent of the voting strength signed their names to fight for the North. Company A of the Seventh Regiment was composed entirely of Hendricks County volunteers, at the Seventh's initial organization. Often companies were filled by neighbors and relatives for the duration of the war. *The History of Hendricks County Indiana*, compiled in 1885, includes the names, rank, and activities of each of the county's sons who served in the Civil War. Some ninety-five pages describe the actions and persons in that conflict.

The War so depleted the adult male population, that many families were hard pressed to continue farming for the war years. Schools were interrupted; businesses suffered, and yet, people assisted at home in any way they could, preparing bandages, caring for returned wounded and sick.

Slowly, after the war ended, the economy of the area recovered, but many memories haunted the former soldiers for a lifetime. The Grand Army of the Republic was organized as a group of fellow Civil War veterans dedicated to honoring the fallen and helping the returned.

Guilford Township Historical Society Collection/Plainfield Public Library

Top: Volunteers in the Civil War from Clayton were believed to have served under Benjamin Harrison in the 70th Infantry.

Bottom: In the reunion of the same regiment, many of the company are gone. The men appear to have tried to reassemble in the same position as the first photo. Their faces show the change war makes on men.

Guilford Township Historical Society Collection/Plainfield Public Library

By the turn of the century, reunions developed more pomp and circumstance, with patriotic speeches, choruses, and lots of American flags and bunting. This is believed to be the fourteenth reunion of the 70th Regiment.

Guilford Township Historical Society Collection/Plainfield Public Library

A book first printed in 1898, and recently reprinted by Nugget Publishers, is an account of his Civil War battles and imprisonment by a Hendricks County native, John V. Hadley. Hadley was the son of one of the earliest founders of the county, Jonathan Hadley who settled in 1822 in Guilford Township. In *Seven Months a Prisoner*, Hadley describes his ordeals with color and deep feeling. The book served as a basis for a popular 1997 novel, *Cold Mountain* by Charles Frazier.

Epidemic

In August of 1873, the town of Lizton, (which had been founded as New Elizabeth) on the banks of the Eel River, in the northwestern township of Union, was struck by an outbreak of cholera. The disease is a vicious and painful one, which can deplete the body of up to four gallons of fluid a day. The first victim was an eighteen-year-old mother, who had just moved to the town

the day before the bacteria-borne disease struck; she was dead by the afternoon of the same day. Within three weeks, twenty-four residents of the town, including the doctor, had been struck down.

The plague decimated the thriving railroad town. The families running the lumber trade moved away; the barrel stave and bumper factory were torn down, and other businesses moved out. Lizton regained its composure, and slowly built itself back up, though never quite to its former level of activity. The oldest existing business in the town, founded in 1910, State Bank of Lizton, is still a thriving independent financial institution with several branches across the county.

Tornado

Portions of the following, comprised an article by the author, Linda Balough, appearing in the *Indianapolis Star* and *Indianapolis News Metro West* edition on March 26, 1998, upon the fiftieth anniversary of the

The Margaret Hodson Collection, Guilford Township Historical Society Collection/Plainfield Public Library

The Margaret Hodson Collection, Guilford Township Historical Society Collection/Plainfield Public Library

Top: This postcard photo of the Vandalia Railroad Station in Coatesville shows what it looked like before the tornado of 1948.

Bottom: Hours after the tornado the same building has been badly damaged.

visitation of the "Coatesville Tornado."

The physical scars, on the land and town, are, for the most part, gone, but the memories of that Good Friday, fifty years ago, are still vivid. References of time, are often measured as "before the tornado, or that happened after the tornado." Hoosiers are stalwart, they recover from these things—they just never forget, what has come to be called the "Coatesville Tornado."

Probably, only the animals sensed the drop in barometric pressure as the warm air along the Wabash River, just south of Terre Haute, met the cold air from Canada. There was no warning as the swirling clouds began to move eastward, and the sky turned greenish. The system picked up energy over Vigo, Clay, and Putnam counties, and then struck with all its fury, in Hendricks County.

Coatesville residents were used to the sound of the "Spirit of St. Louis" evening train, on the Pennsylvania Railroad tracks that ran through town, but the roar at 5:23 PM on March 26, 1948 was not a diesel engine. "I thought it was a train that ran by the house. A few seconds later, I realized that it was no train!" Carlyle Yates, a twenty-four-year-old minister of the Christian Church told the *Indianapolis News* the next day. He hid in the house and when the rampage was over arose to find "nothing left of our brick house or our church next door." Coatesville had been attacked by a deadly force of wind so strong it destroyed the business district, all the churches, and a third of the houses of the town.

That Good Friday evening spawned tornadoes from Oklahoma through Alabama, Missouri, Mississippi, Illinois, Tennessee, and Georgia killing nineteen in those states. The Coatesville twister took fourteen lives as it hit Coatesville, two in Hadley, and two as it ravaged Danville. It gradually spent itself out with touchdowns near Brownsburg in a hailstorm, several strikes in Indianapolis near 71st and Zionsville with more than an inch of rain and finally dissipated as it damaged the 2200 block of Shadeland Avenue.

In Coatesville, "At 12:50 AM the full moon broke through," reported the *Indianapolis News*. But by that time the torrential rains and tornado had left a wake of nearly a foot of water in the streets and severe destruction. Houses were rubble, trees stripped of branches, people were crying and frantically searching for loved ones, and heroes arose to meet the challenge of the disaster.

Hendricks County Historical Society

The walls of the telephone office were gone, but the operator got a call for help through to Dr. Gibbs in Danville and stayed at her post. The five telephone operators in Danville also continued to work in the debris of a partially destroyed telephone building.

Coatesville's only physician, Dr. John Ellet, worked all through the night to help survivors of the storm, although his aunt, uncle, and their grandsons were among the victims killed. Charlie and Margaret Hodson passed out flashlights from their drugstore, and those people not injured in the storm joined Indiana State Police and other groups who came to help restore the town to as much order as possible.

The Indiana State Police cordoned off the town from sightseers as volunteers with bulldozers cleared the streets, and workers looked for whatever could be salvaged. The Red Cross set up in the school to provide food and medical help. Power workers from

Top left: Much of Coatesville is leveled by the tornado.

Top right: An older home on North Washington in Danville lost one wall to the storm.

Bottom: The town of Coatesville after the tornado.

Hendricks County Historical Society

Hendricks County Historical Society

Greencastle restored electricity by 3 AM Sunday. The building housing the Coatesville *Herald* newspaper was virtually destroyed, and publisher Harmon Hathaway and his son were nearly killed. Yet with the help of the Danville *Republican* staff the *Herald* came out the following Thursday with a complete report of the disaster in Coatesville.

Boy Scouts, state governmental agencies—even the Navy—sent help. The *Herald* reported, "Governor Ralph Gates [meeting with local businessmen the following Monday] advised the group what could be done by the state and federal government toward the rehabilitation of the town."

Redbook magazine reported the businessmen accepted no help in rebuilding, and after receiving more than $90,000 in donations to rebuild the town, Mark Hadley, chairman of the Reconstruction Committee refused more saying, "We've no right to spend other people's money on community improvements we could not have afforded ourselves."

A year later the Coatesville *Herald* reported twenty-five of the thirty-seven houses destroyed had been rebuilt. The Sunday April 10, 1949 *Indianapolis Star* read, "There will be an Easter Sunday Service in Coatesville next Sunday the first since 1947 in the newly completed Baptist Church on the site of the 76-year-old frame building." The Methodist Church was completed and the Christian Church nearly so. Most of the businesses were back in operation and a new market bore the name of Tornado Grocery.

The bottom of a silo is all that is recognizable of the Coatesville Elevator.

Hendricks County Historical Society

Names of the deceased

An article by author Betty Bartley in the Hendricks County History Bulletin, Vol. XXVIII Number II, May 1998 published by the Hendricks County Historical Society in Danville lists the victims of that tragedy.

At Coatesville:

Wayne K. Beaman, age 29.

Harry Britton, a resident of Crawfordsville. Mr. Britton was a salesman for the Harris Packing Company and was killed at Elliott's Grocery, where he had stopped on his route.

Janice Coffey, age 16. She and her boyfriend, Harry Eugene Rumley, age 22, were buried under the rubble of the Fuson home on North Milton. They were planning to be married in the spring.

continues overleaf

Right: More destruction in Coatesville after the tornado.

Below: The Lakin Block in Coatesville remained much the same from the early 1900s until the tornado of 1948 demolished much of the town.

Hendricks County Historical Society

Guilford Township Historical Society Collection/Plainfield Public Library

Frank and Lottie Ellett, husband and wife, both age 60. Mr. Ellett had been postmaster at Coatesville since 1933. They and their two grandsons, Richard Allen "Dickie" Ellett, age 7 and Russell Lloyd White, age 3, were killed at the grandparents home. White's sister, Rose, lost an arm. Russell and Rose's mother, Mary Lou Ellett White, and another sister, Thelma Jean, were in another part of town, unhurt. The children's father, Eugene White had been killed in an auto accident a month before Russell was born.

Julia Lawrence, age 35. Wife of Fred Lawrence. Her two daughters, Julia Clare and Annette, were injured.

Frank Grimes, age 45. Son of Marion and Clara Harlan Grimes.

Perry Knight, age 36. Killed at the Gulf Station.

Wayne Pursell, and his wife, Muriel Pursell, both 37, were trying to escape in their car when it was crushed by a collapsing brick building. Russell Siddons, a passenger in the back seat, was injured.

Victor Leroy Wise, age 48. Suffered a fatal heart attack upon hearing that his grandson, Dickie Ellett, had been killed.

Hendricks County Historical Society

At Hadley:
Grace D. Hadley, age 71.

Fletcher Hartsaw, killed when he sought refuge in the general store.

At Danville:
Miss Jessie Dooley, age 71. Died in an Indianapolis hospital from injuries sustained when her brick house on West Main was demolished by the tornado.

Donald Eugene Howard, age 14. The only child of Homer and Dorothy Roberts Howard, he was blown from his parents' home and struck in the head by flying debris. Eight of his classmates served as pallbearers at his funeral.

Top left: Looking east on Main Street in Danville after the storm.

Top right: This house on West Main was purchased by the Catholic Church after the tornado. It was later used as the rectory.

Bottom: The former Masonic building on West Main in Danville lost its third story to the storm.

Hendricks County Historical Society

Hendricks County Historical Society

7 Schools

EDUCATION WAS VALUED HIGHLY among the settlers of Hendricks County, though in the early days the conditions in which lessons were taught, were not conducive to ready learning.

Early schools were floorless, log houses with a heap of logs burning in one end to provide warmth. Glass was much too precious a commodity to use in a school, so windows were cut out of the log walls, and oiled paper furnished light but supplied meager resistance to the outside elements. Children sat on stools so high their feet dangled above the floor, and the teacher always had a switch of birch with which to encourage any reluctant student to higher efforts.

The first schools were built in 1823, only three years after the first whites settled on the banks of White Lick Creek. One was a half mile south of

Frame school houses, such as this structure at Pittsboro, were used throughout the county. Many were later replaced with brick schools. The students and their teacher, W. F. Franklin, gathered outside on a winter day for a photograph. Note the woodpile, to the right, that was used to fuel the stove that heated the building.

Guilford Township Historical Society Collection/Plainfield Public Library

what is now Cartersburg, and the other was on Thomas Lockhart's land in Guilford Township.

By 1885 there were 108 school houses of which 54 were brick. In the school year of 1884–1885 there were 5,836 students, and the 147 teachers in the county drew a daily wage of $2.36 according to an account written by T. R. Gilleland in 1885 in *History of Hendricks County Indiana*. He proudly proclaimed, "The log cabin has passed away, and the frame or brick building has taken its place. . . . We now have the tasteful edifice supplied with all the educational appliances that utility and educational economy can furnish."

The reason for so many schools in the county traces back to the state legislature of 1852. That body passed a law charging the township trustee with providing education convenient to the population. Districts were

set up in each township, and each district could decide for itself how much tax money to raise for education. There were so many schools, it became harder to find enough teachers, giving rise to the popularity of normal, or teachers colleges which produced, in eighteen weeks, teachers ready to take on the education of all the students in a one-room schoolhouse.

School sessions in the 1850s were of short duration. In *Travels in Indiana 1679–1961*, published by the Indiana Historical Bureau, Leander M. Campbell, a teacher in the district schools of Hendricks County, tells that he took up teaching at a school "three miles from Pittsborough, and about three miles from Brownsburg . . . to up to 40 students" in early May. He said he completed the school after a few weeks, and "collected all but 40 cents" and began searching for another. He began teaching at Belleville

Hendricks County Historical Society

Hendricks County Historical Society

Above: District schools were officially identified by township and district number. Unofficially, some colorful nicknames were used by nearby citizens. Brown Township District School No. 5 was locally known as the "Sambo School." It is thought the title came from the name of an early teacher, Samuel Sambough.

Left: As the population declined in some rural districts, keeping the smaller schools open became a financial burden, and new, larger buildings were used to serve larger numbers of students. The Cartersburg School, built in 1897, was the result of the consolidation of several Liberty Township districts.

The Ash Grove School, located in Guilford Township, was started in 1898. By that time, African-American children attended district schools along with white children. Before 1869, schools were open to whites only. That year, a law was passed requiring the establishment of "Colored District Schools" wherever there was a sufficient number of students. In 1877, the law was modified to allow integrated schools.

Guilford Township Historical Society Collection/Plainfield Public Library

on August 4 after he had "stuck the price up a little."

Finally in the early 1900s, school district leaders realized it would be cheaper to bring the students to the schools than try to continue to bring schools to the students. They began to consolidate the districts. Horse-drawn school hacks, and later motorized buses, began to take the pupils to the centralized schools. Eventually the schools were consolidated into township systems and later, some townships and towns further combined into community school corporations.

In the late 1800s state-wide standards began to be established for the education of Indiana children. In the 1890s a law was passed requiring schools to teach the harmful effects of alcohol, stimulants, and narcotics. A typical textbook included warnings about the use of tobacco and the overuse of tea and coffee.

The Central Academy at Plainfield was a Quaker secondary school operating from 1881 until 1919. It offered courses of science, English, Latin, German, history, mathematics, and other fields of study to whites and blacks alike, and to both males and females, yet there were separate stairways for girls and boys. Students were primarily from the Quaker communities in Morgan, Hendricks, and Marion counties, but some came from as far away as Oklahoma and North Carolina.

The Hadley Industrial School was dedicated on August 23, 1894. This educational facility for underprivileged or orphaned girls was established by Addison and Martha Hadley, to teach the young women to be self-supporting. Danville Judge John V. Hadley spoke at the dedication, "No higher service can be rendered society than a proper preparation of girls to assume the natural and conventional responsibilities that will

HADLEY INDUSTRIAL SCHOOL.

The Women's Christian Temperance Union supported the Hadley Industrial School for underprivileged girls, helping them learn the domestic arts and farming techniques.

The former Danville Academy building became the home of Central Normal College in 1878.

Hendricks County Historical Society

come to them . . . housekeeping, cookery, sewing, music, and a general knowledge of horticulture and dairying enter as essentially as grammar and arithmetic to the proper equipment of a young woman to be queen of a family."

Sometime after 1829, a seminary for young women was established at Danville. The building and additions were built from timbers cut and brick made and fired on the site, at the corner of Wayne and Main Streets. After being purchased by the Danville Methodist Church, and another building added to the campus, the school became Danville Academy—a much more broadly based educational facility which ran

successfully for a time. However, by 1868 the Civil War had decimated the number of male students and staff, and the academy was closed and one of the buildings used as the Methodist Church. In 1878 several Danville businessmen bought the campus and offered it as a new site for the Central Normal College, then located in Ladoga, Indiana.

Central Normal College had been established two years earlier by Warren Darst and William F. Harper. When the enrollment jumped from forty to nearly three hundred in those two years, Harper needed larger facilities and planned to move the school at the end of the spring semester. When rumors spread that some of the people from Ladoga were planning to get a court order to stop the move, Harper enlisted help. Before dawn on May 10, nearly fifty buggies and wagons carried equipment, books, and belongings to the new location in Danville, and classes began the next day.

The two teachers and the few students who remained at Ladoga continued to operate the school at Ladoga on a much smaller scale for several years.

The new Central Normal College at Danville went forward under the hand of Professor Franklin P. Adams after the disappearance of Professor Harper (see sidebar). When Adams died suddenly at the age of thirty, the school staff petitioned the court to allow his wife, Ora, to become the full owner of the college, going against the law allowing a wife to inherit only a third of the estate of a man who died without a will. It was extremely rare for a woman to head a co-educational institution at that time, but she successfully operated the school for nearly ten years.

Central Normal continued to produce teachers and other graduates, as well as provide the center of the cultural community for Danville and the county, until its demise in 1946, when it was purchased by the Northern Diocese of the Episcopal Church. The school curriculum was restructured, and the name changed to Canterbury College.

Hendricks County Historical Society

Professor Charles Allen Hargrave was the "grand old man" of Central Normal College. He joined the faculty in 1883 and was an important influence on the school until his death in 1927.

The auditorium of Central Normal's Chapel Hall was filled to witness a graduation ceremony in the 1900s. The hall was also used for a daily assembly, where professors lectured, and sometimes read articles on current events, to the student body.

Hendricks County Historical Society

Unfortunately, the financial structure of that school disintegrated, and the college closed its doors in 1951. The site still advances the education of Hendricks County youth, however. It is the current location of the Danville Middle School and two of the many buildings that were eventually part of the Central Normal College, the gymnasium and Hargrave Hall, are portions of the current building.

Avon resident May Loy began her course at Central Normal the week after her graduation from high school in 1914. She was following a tradition, since her mother and father, Ida and James Comer had met at the college when they attended in 1890. The 102-year-old lady recalls the teaching methods Mrs. Olcott taught her during her eighteen-week course to become a teacher.

"We let the students find out for themselves." Loy taught students at the Shiloh School in Washington Township and gives this example of allowing her pupils to discover their way to an education.

A wide-angle view shows the campus of Central Normal College as it looked in 1915. The new Science Hall, at the far right, was later renamed Hargrave Hall, in honor of Professor Charles Allen Hargrave.

Hendricks County Historical Society

The Founder of Central Normal College

William French Harper was born in 1854 near New Winchester in Hendricks County. At the age of sixteen he received his teacher's license and taught at schools near Amo and Clayton.

Hendricks County Historical Society

Wanting to further his education, he enrolled in National Normal at Lebanon, Ohio, graduating in 1873. The following year he was hired as principal instructor in that school's Teacher's Department.

In September of 1876, he and Warren Darst founded the very successful Central Normal College at Ladoga, Indiana.

Six months after the college was removed to Danville the twenty-four-year-old Professor Harper disappeared. No word was heard of him until nearly a year later, when his family received a telegram from Wyoming. He claimed he had been kidnapped and abandoned in a camp of Ute Indians. Upon his return to Danville, he resigned and turned control of the college over to Franklin P. Adams.

Harper died in Los Angeles in 1930.

Wm. F. Harper founded
Central Normal College.

"I had them measure the circumference of a pie pan, and then the diameter, and write it down on a chart. Their homework was to use their mother's measuring line and measure her pans, pie pans—anything round—and then measure across the item and write down both figures on their charts. Some did a half dozen things and some filled the page with records. The next day I had them divide each circumference number by the distance across, or diameter. As they kept coming up with the same results of the circumference being about three and one

The Central Normal Class of 1909 had a group photo taken on a hillside near the park. During that time period, enrollment at the school averaged between eight hundred and one thousand students.

Hendricks County Historical Society

What is NORMAL?

The term Normal School originated in France in the early 1800s. It comes from the French word for model or rule. The purpose of a normal school was to give rules for teaching.

Teacher training was not widely practiced in the United States until the mid-1800s. The first state normal school opened in Massachusetts in 1839.

In the Midwest, normal schools developed when the district school system was started in the 1850s. In each county there could be over a hundred district schools. The need for qualified teachers was answered by the normal school.

The Indiana State Normal School at Terre Haute opened in 1870. (Later to become Indiana State University.) Across the state dozens of private normal schools appeared in the 1870s and 1880s.

One of the most successful private normal schools was Danville's Central Normal College. It has been estimated Central Normal produced seventy-five thousand graduates.

A survey conducted in 1930 of the thirty-seven teacher-training schools in Indiana, showed Central Normal ranked sixth in the number of teachers graduated and third in the number of graduates who became principals or superintendents of schools.

A tabulation of the alumni of teacher-training colleges listed in "Who's Who in America" during the 1930s ranked Central Normal as second among the graduates from Indiana schools.

seventh times the diameter, they began to look at me. I told them there was a rule that said that is true every time you make that measurement—they had proven the rule. Seeing that look, when they began to catch on, is the joy of teaching."

In 1867, Governor Oliver P. Morton had the House of Refuge for Delinquent Boys established and built, a mile south and west from Plainfield. The institution has experienced many changes in name and educational structure, but preparing young men for life outside the grounds has always been the goal. Charlton High School was established within the institution and early lessons included blacksmithing, plumbing, carpentry, and shoe making. The farming program was discontinued in the 1970s and education has been revolutionized with the use of computers. The latest name change was effected in 1998, adopting Plainfield Juvenile Correction Facility in favor of the long lived Indiana Boys School.

On some of the acreage formerly belonging to the Indiana Boys School, a new facility was established in the 1960s called the Indiana Youth Center. This facility was designed to house young men fifteen to twenty-six who had never been incarcerated before. Arthur Campbell High School was founded within this facility which, to date, is the only accredited prison high school in Indiana. It holds accreditation within the North Central Association of Colleges and Secondary Schools. The Youth Center's name was changed, also in 1998, to Plainfield Correctional Facility.

Above: The superintendent's home on the grounds of the Indiana Boys School still stands today.

Left: Dinner time at the Indiana Boys School.

Guilford Township Historical Society Collection/Plainfield Public Library

Hendricks County Historical Society

The Dover School, located in Liberty Township, was said to provide an exceptional education, and was known in the area as the "Harvard" of Hendricks County schools.

Hendricks County Historical Society

Left: The brick school house was the most popular style in the Midwest. The White School, in Eel River Township, was an elegant example. The teacher, Hiram Storm, was a veteran of the Civil War, who lost a leg in battle at the age of seventeen.

Below: Many of the small district school buildings which once dotted the county are gone, but some have been converted to homes. This one used to be the Hebron School near Indiana 75 and U.S. 40.

Guilford Township Historical Society Collection/Plainfield Public Library

Hendricks County Historical Society

Above: The old school ties held strong for many years after the students left the classroom for the world. The first students to attend Tilden school, built in 1885, appear dwarfed by the large brick structure.

Right: When a reunion of the Tilden students was held fifty-four years later, a second group photo was taken in front of the school. The teacher, W. F. Franklin, appears in both pictures: to the right in the doorway in 1895, and seated in the center of the front row in 1941, with his hat on his lap.

Hendricks County Historical Society

In the early 1900s, class portraits were taken on the steps of the school, as seen in this example from Brownsburg in 1910.

Guilford Township Historical Society Collection/Plainfield Public Library

Top: An awareness of the importance of exercise for both sexes had the schools include sports for girls as well as boys. The Amo girls' basketball team wore uniforms that reflected the beginnings of reform in women's clothing. Back row: Sadie O'Neal, Ruby Halfhill, Marcia Morris, and Mary Snyder. Front row: Alice Cox, Edith Atkins, and Elsie Garrison.

Bottom: Informal play became structured competition in high schools during the 1900s. County and state tourneys were held to select the "winningest" teams. In 1906, the Amo football team won the High School Athletics Association championship. Back row, left to right: Wesley Lambert, Forrest Kelley, Mervyn Hung, Frank O'Neal, Thomas Masters, and Sam Cooprider; middle: Vern McAnninch; front: Bob Ewing, Joe Steers, Drassa Pruitt, Glendon Kelley, and Henry Vickery.

Hendricks County Historical Society

Hendricks County Historical Society

Guilford Township Historical Society Collection/Plainfield Public Library

Hendricks County Historical Society

Top: Athletic programs became a means of promoting school pride in the early 1900s. The Pittsboro basketball team proudly wore their school initial on their uniforms.

Bottom: Football grew in popularity in the early 1900s. Despite the fact that it was banned at some colleges, due to serious injuries and some deaths resulting from rough play, it was included as an extra-curricular activity at most county schools. The Brownsburg High School football team of 1911 posed for a group photo.

Guilford Township Historical Society Collection/Plainfield Public Library

Top: The girls of Central Academy in Plainfield posed for their 1898 class photograph. Emma Dillon, Geneva Vaught, Effie Black, Amanda Phillips and Sibbie Henley are in the first row; second row ladies are Ella Hadley, May Merrit, Florence Hanna, Edith Raines and Jessie Swindler. (Listed right to left.)

Bottom: Graduation from a school of higher education such as this 1904 class from the Plainfield Central Academy was treated with much ceremony. The women wore beautifully fashioned white dresses and the men wore their best starched collars with their wool suits.

Hendricks County Historical Society

Left: Members of the community pitched in to help with the construction of a new school at Amo in 1899.

Below: As the smaller school districts were closed, students were transferred by "school hack" to the larger, centrally located schools. Consolidation reversed the goal of the District School System: to bring the school to the student.

Hendricks County Historical Society

Guilford Township Historical Society Collection/Plainfield Public Library

Guilford Township Historical Society Collection/Plainfield Public Library

Above: Edward Barrett was superintendent of the Belleville Academy beginning in 1883. Two of his former pupils, John M. Pritchard and Arthur Craven, wrote that they thought he was the "Ideal teacher" when they sent him this picture of the three of them in 1938. The Belleville Academy was established in 1853. The building later served as a public school and was torn down in 1964.

Right: Jonathan Rigdon, a CNC graduate, joined the faculty in 1885, and served as president twice, from 1900 to 1903 and from 1918 to 1929. He was the author of a series of grammar textbooks published in Danville and used throughout the state.

Hendricks County Historical Society

Hendricks County Historical Society

Above: Faculty and students at Central Normal posed for a portrait in the 1880s. Charles A. Hargrave (fourth from right, front row) and J. A. Joseph (far left, back row) were students who later served as the college's president. CeDora Lieuellen (fifth from left, front row) was a faculty member who became the first woman attorney in the county.

Left: Dr. Joseph Tingley of Central Normal was a scientist and artist. He painted several oil portraits of faculty members. He also experimented with the telephone in the late 1870s, connecting his house to one of the other professor's.

DePauw University Archives and Special Collections

Guilford Township Historical Society Collection/Plainfield Public Library

8 Agriculture

Scenes of corn harvesting at the Boy's School show boys selecting ears of corn from the current harvest to supply seed for the next year's crop.

LIKE MOST OF THE AREAS IN THE OLD Northwest Territory, the dominant business of the 1800s and early 1900s in Hendricks County was agriculture.

Pioneer farmers who, at first only provided sustenance for themselves and a few other settlers, increased their land and began to feed more livestock and grow more crops for bigger markets.

Early farmers put fences around their crops fields to keep the roaming livestock OUT. Indiana was a woody open range in summer as the animals foraged for themselves. When they needed to, farmers sorted out which animal was whose from a registry kept in the county recorder's office describing the markings they made on each animal, usually slashes or "V" shapes in one or both of the animal's ears.

127

Hendricks County Historical Society

Today's practice of confinement feeding was not widely used in the early 1900s. Barred Plymouth Rock chickens socially mixed with young jersey calves on a Clay Township farm around 1910.

As the number of livestock multiplied, that system became unwieldy and fences were finally built to keep the family's animals IN.

Hogs

Hogs were very important and efficient animals for the early settlers. They ate anything, didn't mind the mucky soil in many parts of the county, and did well at caring for themselves in adverse situations. They provided meat at home and were about the only "crop" that could be taken to market.

As they cleared more land, Hendricks County settlers could grow abundant corn in the rich soil, but the question was how to ship it to other markets? Farmers reasoned they could feed the corn to their tough, long-legged hogs and "walk it out."

In the late fall, fattened hogs were driven in herds along the National Road and down other trails to slaughter houses in the river towns of Madison and Cincinnati about a hundred miles away. The trail boss on horseback and six to eight drovers on foot, would usher the herd of two to three hundred or more hogs along the still-muddy trail—frozen ground would cut the hogs' feet. Many taverns along the way were not just resting places for the travelers, but would have stock lots for feeding and bedding down the weary animals. The train boss could expect a bed; but the drovers, with boots and clothing thick with hog-churned mud, could only find accommodations on the kitchen floor.

The slaughter houses ran only during the cold months, and winter in Cincinnati was likely to insult the nose as well as hinder slow traffic. An account published in the *Brookville American* newspaper, in November of 1834, speculates there were upwards of thirty thousand hogs making their way through that town to market in Cincinnati. Once the hogs were delivered, the drovers walked the trails back home, but Cincinnati residents were left with the tumult and the aroma. The August 1994 edition of *Indiana Historian*, a publication of the Indiana History Bureau, quotes a letter from an Englishwoman, Mrs. Trollope, who lived in Cincinnati from 1827 to 1831. On an attempt to stroll to a nearby park, she and a friend encountered a brook red with pig blood from an upstream slaughterhouse. She adds that, when crossing the street, " . . . the chances were five hundred to one against my reaching the shady side without brushing by a snout or two, fresh dripping from the kennel. . . . [we] were greeted by odors that I will not describe, and which I heartily hope my readers cannot imagine . . ."

Hendricks County Historical Society

When the geese began to fly south and the first cold weather appeared, the neighborhood hog butchering would begin. Men and women joined in the work of preparing the meat, which would be salted, smoked, or ground, and the fat was made into lard. A scene from a Washington Township farm shows the hogs hung, ready to be washed, dressed, and halved.

At one time, the donkey played an important role in agriculture. The males, called "jacks," and female "jennies," were crossbred with horses to produce mules. The American Standard Jackstock was the largest of the breed, often weighing over one thousand pounds. A fine example of Jackstock was photographed on the Cecil Prebster farm near Brownsburg, with young Maurice Prebster on board.

Hendricks County Historical Society

Horses and mules

While the first animals to haul wagons to Indiana were probably oxen, Hendricks County residents preferred horses and mules to work the farms. These sturdy animals provided the power to clear and plant fields and then furnished transportation to town. As the farmer grew more affluent, he might acquire specialized animals, draft types for heavy pulling, "chunks," or light draft horses for regular farm work and more lively saddle and livery horses for Saturday's "goin' to town" or the Sunday trip to church.

Some farmers began to breed fine horses and, in the late 1800s, Hendricks County horse farms provided some excellent additions to the sport of harness racing. Nearly a hundred years later, in 1973, Navajo,

a Hendricks County thoroughbred born on Windswept Farms near Danville, raced against the famous Secretariat in the Kentucky Derby.

Cattle

Dairy cows were an important part of the family farm. At one time, over one hundred dairies operated in Hendricks County, furnishing wholesome milk and rich cream for butter and cheese. One farm produced up to twenty-two thousand pounds of milk a day from five hundred milk cows. The Bottema Farms, founded in 1900, once covered over one thousand acres and eight farms where Interstate 70 now intersects Ind. 267 at the south edge of Plainfield. One of the Bottema prize Holstein-Friesian bulls, Fond Memory, brought a world record

Guilford Township Historical Society Collection/Plainfield Public Library

price of $280,000 in 1975, only a few years before the farms were closed down and much of the land sold for development. Few dairy farmers remain in the county.

Beef cattle are still abundant in Hendricks County. Many farmers in the county also work off the farm, so the labor-intensive dairy herd had to give way to beef production.

At one time, poultry was a larger business in the county than now, but it, too, requires more daily manpower than many Hendricks County farmers can afford.

Crops

As more of the heavily forested land was cleared, Hendricks County farmers began to grow more of the crops typical of the "west"—corn, wheat, oats, and hay.

The Jackson-Havens Poultry House operated at Clayton from 1902 to 1968. Pictured is the first carload of chickens shipped from Clayton. By 1925, the company recorded $450,000 in sales.

One unusual farm crop was introduced to Hendricks County in 1886, when a Civil War veteran named Adrian A. Parsons imported "soja" seed from Japan to grow on his farm.

What we now call soybeans, was originally raised as a coffee substitute; but Parsons believed the plant had greater value as a feed for livestock.

During the 1890s, Parsons wrote numerous articles on the soybean as a farm crop for a number of farm publications and drew the attention of the United States Department of Agriculture, which began to study his crops. By the 1900s, Parsons and his sons were growing hundreds of acres of soybeans. He even developed a new variety named "Mikado," that produced more beans, with pods that were less likely to shatter before maturity.

Soon, many of the farmers who had ridiculed Parsons for experimenting with the odd crop, were devoting much of their own fields to raising the beans.

Today, the value of the "soja" seed imported by A. A. Parsons has expanded beyond livestock feed to produce thousands of products and goes to markets around the world. In 1997, according to the Indiana Soybean Growers Association, Indiana's soybean crop was estimated at $1,556 million, and that same year the U.S. exported over $1,109 million in soybeans to the rest of the

Adrian A. Parsons, shown here with his son, World War I veteran Chet, was a driving force in making soybeans the profitable crop it is today. Chet (born 1887) had just returned from World War I when this shot was taken. The war had taken his youngest son Frank. Adrian had nearly lost his life near Franklin, Tennessee in the Civil War, where he lay for four days in an abandoned log cabin before Union troops found him.

Hendricks County Historical Society

Hendricks County Historical Society

world, including Japan, where Parsons got his first experimental seeds.

Other grains like oats, wheat, and corn, were staples for man and animal alike. Corn was a main crop on almost every farm. Nearly every stream had a mill and in the 1800s people usually brought the grain and visited while their flour or corn meal was being prepared. As the grain farms became even more productive with the addition of insecticides and commercial fertilizers, grain elevators began to dot the countryside, particularly in the railroad towns. The tall, metal cylinders served as a storage place for the grain until it could be poured into railroad cars and hauled away to distant markets. Now, some farms are so large and productive, they have their own storage systems and the farmer waits for just the right market before selling.

A building for elevating, storing, and discharging grain was known as an elevator. The Fowler elevator at Pittsboro, shown in the early 1900s, was the tallest building in the area.

In an excerpt from a book by her husband, "White, Red, Black, Sketches of American Society in the United States During the Visit of Their Guests," 2 Vols. New York, 1853, from Vol. 2, ppg 5–13, an account appearing in "Travel Accounts of Indiana," 1679–1961 (pg. 203), the wife of a visiting dignitary from Hungary relates an explanation of the word, "Hoosiers." She was Teresa Pulsky, wife of politician and writer Ferencz Pulsky and was a guest of the governor in 1852. "Governor Wright is a type of the Hoosiers, and justly proud to be one of them. I asked him wherefrom his people had got this name. He told me that 'Hoosa' is the Indian name for maize; the principal produce of the state."

Hendricks County Historical Society

Maize or corn has been king in Indiana since the settlers first arrived.

Guilford Township Historical Society Collection/Plainfield Public Library

Wagons loaded with bushels of tomatoes were brought to canning factories for processing.

Many towns in Hendricks County had canneries in the late 1800s, some through the middle 1900s. These businesses would accept the fresh tomatoes or other "truck" crop and process and can the vegetables for sale in the groceries of Indianapolis or beyond. While many farms further north in Indiana still grow tomatoes for canning, the farmers in Hendricks County have nearly all switched to less labor-intensive grain production.

Hendricks County Historical Society

Mules, a cross between a jackass and a horse, were common on most farms in the county. They served as a reliable source of power for pulling wagons and plows.

Hendricks County Historical Society

Guilford Township Historical Society Collection/Plainfield Public Library

Top: Courses in agriculture were part of the curriculum in Hendricks County in the early 1900s. Even the inmates at the Boy's School at Plainfield were taught how crops were raised and harvested.

Bottom: Families and friends often gathered to "Sugar Down" the sap they collected from tapping their maple trees in the early spring. Here Sam Holderman and friends from Indianapolis tap the trees on his picnic grounds in Cartersburg and prepare to cook down the sweet sap into maple syrup.

Hendricks County Historical Society

"Thrashing," or threshing, was the process of removing grain, such as oats and wheat, from the straw. The "thrashing ring" was the crew who performed the series of tasks necessary. Even with the advent of the steam engine, it took as many as twenty to thirty men and boys, as well as women and girls, to accomplish the work. A neighborhood "thrashing" was photographed on the Christie farm, between Rockville Road and Hadley, in Marion Township.

Hendricks County Historical Society

Hendricks County Historical Society

Top: The farm dog earned his living by herding livestock and protecting them from predators. This dog took time from his labors to pose for photographer O. P. Phillips near Amo.

Bottom: Poultry of all varieties could be found on Hendricks County farms. The Prairie Farmer's Guide of 1920 listed thirty-six breeders of ducks, geese, and turkeys. Ida Logue is shown feeding ducks on a farm near Amo.

Clayton Milling Company, owned by L. C. Vanarsdell and Arthur Shaw, was built in 1903 to handle the grains pouring in from the successful farms in the area. Flour not used locally, was sent out under the names of Life, Our Pride, and Harvest Queen at the rate of about three boxcar loads a month.

Industrial Souvenir of Hendricks County, State of Indiana

Hendricks County Historical Society

9 Businesses

THE EARLIEST EXPLORERS TO PASS through the wilderness we now call Hendricks County were almost completely self reliant taking their food, shelter, and clothing from the countryside. Later, when pioneers set up permanent homes, nearly every early family in Hendricks County cared for livestock and tended a garden, made their own butter, clothes, furniture, and tools. But self reliant as they were, some things were not easily made at home. Entrepreneurial "pack peddlers" carried wares into the new settlements on their backs, and bartered with the widely scattered settlers for the goods they needed.

Later "huckster wagons," at first horse-drawn and later motorized, plied the streets of town and the backroads to sell pans, fabrics, tools, and whatever else the market demanded. In

Two brothers, Roger and James Jones lived on the County Farm in the late 1940s with their mother and father. They wanted to make a record of their experiences, and in 1998 gave the following oral history interview to Betty Bartley, president of the Hendricks County Historical Society.

Roger: "I can remember the old huckster coming around . . . As soon as you stepped in the huckster, they had them long, black licorice hanging. You got about three of them for a penny or something like that. Mother would take scissors and cut and put them in a fruit jar, and when we got down to two the huckster was coming. We got one a day."

James: "The huckster was a wonderful thing. They were like a general store on wheels, usually an old bus or something converted . . . And they had everything in there. You could buy a pair of coveralls to your food staples. Mom would always buy us a banana, off the stalk and powdered donuts, and a little half-pint jar of chocolate milk. I remember saying, 'If I ever get rich, I'm going to eat all the bananas and all the chocolate milk I want!'"

Roger: "If you didn't have money, you took a chicken or maybe a dozen eggs [to trade] and you couldn't carry the groceries back to the house."

James: "It was almost like going to town; I mean town coming to you. It was exciting. He carried a little bit of just about anything you would want. And if it was something special, you'd just tell him and he'd make a note of it and the next time he came by, he'd have it. So they really did a service to rural people, because lots of people didn't have any means to get to town. We certainly enjoyed it."

Pack peddlers gave way to huckster wagons as the roads in Hendricks County improved enough for wagon traffic. Hucksters operated in the county up until the 1940s and very early 1950s. In the old days they were often Jewish men looking for a place to settle down. F. V. Beeler was photographed at Friendswood in Guilford Township in about 1910 with his fine huckster wagon.

The History of Hendricks County, 1914-1976, pg. 639

Industrial Souvenir of Hendricks County, State of Indiana

Guilford Township Historical Society Collection/Plainfield Public Library

Hendricks County Historical Society

Mills were one of the first type of businesses set up in the county. At first serving to process local grains, they later became outlets for a variety of agricultural supplies. The Klondike Mill at Danville began operation the year that gold was discovered in the Yukon. At one time it was one of the most successful businesses in the county.

It took a team of four horses to haul this huge walnut log to the Cartersburg Lumber Company in 1913.

A ready supply of lumber was needed by a growing county population. The Frank Horn lumber business at Amo supplied building material for the Clay Township area.

Hendricks County some of the huckster wagons still made their rounds in the 1940s and 1950s.

As communities grew, early businesses supplied their needs. Along the streams and rivers were saw mills, flour mills, and woolen mills. Later, tile factories and brickyards made use of the Indiana clay. Tanneries and traders stores appeared.

The early Hendricks County residents were a gregarious lot. They often arrived in groups from North Carolina and Kentucky, and settled near one another. Towns quickly sprang up, with stores to provide some of the more sophisticated products, as the settlements prospered. Some offered wallpaper, carpeting, and furniture.

By the late 1800s undertakers instead of family members handled more funerals. In

Right: Every town's "Main Street" was the center of commerce. In Brownsburg, the intersection of Main and Green Streets boasted brick business buildings.

Below: Many undertakers operated companion businesses, most often furniture making. Wm. F. Evans operated his undertaking and furniture ventures from this building in Brownsburg. He arrived in 1900, worked for I. C. Tolle and then became the sole proprietor.

Hendricks County Historical Society

Industrial Souvenir of Hendricks County, State of Indiana

the early 1900s, funeral homes appeared, replacing the old custom of having services in the family parlor. The funeral director became as central a figure to the community as a banker or attorney. Early undertakers often shared that business with furniture making, and while most have split into separate businesses; one building in Coatesville, now owned by Dan Hays, was built in the 1860s by William Lakin and still connects the furniture store with the funeral parlor Hays also operates.

Soon ready-to-wear clothing stores featured the latest fashions. Millinery shops offered milady new hats for purchase, or would redesign their old ones to fit the newest eastern fashion. Dry goods stores and drugstores sprang up on corners, and groceries and general stores offered canned

Millinery, the fine art of making women's hats, was one of the few businesses that women could enter. Minnie M. Hadley's shop in Plainfield could make new hats to order or redesign old ones to suit the latest fashion.

goods, produce from other areas, and cookware, along with hardware and hatchets for the farmstead.

When an area grew prosperous, banks were established. The First National Bank of Danville was founded during the Civil War on September 23, 1863. It was the fourth bank in Indiana and enjoyed immediate success. In recent years, that bank was bought out, and is now known as Huntington Bank. Only two of the banks born in Hendricks County remain operating under their original name. The State Bank of Lizton, established in 1910, now has branches in Pittsboro, Zionsville, Brownsburg, and Lebanon. North Salem State Bank was founded in 1923, and also operates from its second location in Danville.

The earliest doctors in the county were often self taught. Isaac Furnas came to Indiana in 1826 and became a successful

Industrial Souvenir of Hendricks County, State of Indiana

Established in 1891, the North Salem Bank was a private institution, with George B. Davis as cashier and principle stockholder. It later became affiliated with the National Bank system and was reestablished as the North Salem State Bank.

farmer. He also became a doctor when his wife took ill and he ordered a book on medicine. Furnas successfully treated her and subsequently found himself in demand by Hoosiers far and wide to attend to their injuries and diseases.

One good thing that came from the Civil War was the beginnings of sterilization of sick rooms and operating utensils. Sanitary Commissions promoted cleanliness and more healthful conditions during the war. Later, as many of the same people became public health officials, they brought sewer services and better protection of water supplies to many communities, lowering the instances of many diseases.

In the early twentieth century, the discoveries of antibiotics, development

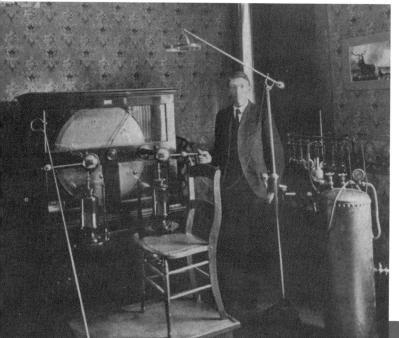

Industrial Souvenir of Hendricks County, State of Indiana

Dr. C. B. Thomas conducted his practice from his office in Brownsburg in the early 1900s. The use of magnets, electricity, and other unique procedures were popular for treating many of the ailments of the times. It appears Dr. Thomas was a doctor who believed in the merits of the innovative devices.

of vaccines, and advances in medical equipment also improved the health of the people in the county.

By the early 1900s, most treatment and surgeries were still done at home or at the doctor's offices in town. If hospitalization was required, patients went outside the county to Lebanon, Greencastle, or Indianapolis. Several attempts were made to bring a hospital to the county, but it wasn't until 1962 that Hendricks County Hospital (now known as Hendricks Community Hospital) was built on county-owned property in Danville.

Newspapers in nearly every town faithfully, or sometimes, intentionally prejudicially, recorded the events of the times. One newspaper which began as the Danville Advertiser established in 1847, is still operating today. It underwent many name changes, but The Republican, located in Danville, has never missed an issue since its inception, and still resides in the same building on the square it has occupied since 1897.

Two other newspapers are now widely circulated in Hendricks County. The Hendricks County Flyer was born in 1965, and bought out several papers to become the most widely distributed publication in the county, and in March of 1999, was itself bought out by Thompson Newspapers, an international publishing firm.

The Indianapolis Star and Indianapolis News combined in 1995, and established a Metro West bureau office in Avon, which serves both Hendricks and Morgan counties.

It was not until 1962 that Hendricks County citizens had their own hospital, located at Danville. Today there are branches of the hospital in other areas of the county.

Hendricks County Historical Society

In 1938, residents were very pleased with the mural painted by Gail Martin which graced the lobby wall over the post-master's office door at the newly built Danville Post Office.

Photo by Linda Balough

The mural in the Danville post office.

A mural in the Danville post office was painted as part of a WPA type of program for artists. Murals were commissioned all over the U.S. for public buildings, and especially for post offices. In 1938 Gail W. Martin, an artist, who grew up on a farm, and frequently visited his in-laws farm near Franklin, Indiana, was awarded the commission to paint a mural over the postmaster's door in the Danville post office. The result was a scene at the community water pump, of citizens gathering to quench their thirst and fill their jugs for work in the hay fields. When a new post office was built, the building was sold in 1998 to the county, and now is being renovated to be used as county offices. The mural remains Postal Service property and will stay in the building, on loan, for as long as the painting is cared for, and available for public viewing.

As some towns grew in size, municipal water works became a necessity, not only for households, but for the local fire department. Danville's water works were the direct result of a disastrous fire on the west side of the square in 1891. This photograph shows Jonathan S. Marshall (left) and an unidentified co-worker alongside one of the town's artesian wells.

Hendricks County Historical Society

Water was a source of attraction and income for some of the early towns. Danville's higher elevation than the surrounding county lands, gave the locals reason to believe the water from its wells were superior. "You'd never get sick from that water," was an early claim.

One town cashed in on the water from an area rich with Indian relics, that boasted as many as fifteen springs of pure, clear water. It was obvious, the Indians had found the place to be as attractive a gathering place as the white population, around Cartersburg, did in later years. The lovely cove known as Cartersburg Magnetic Springs was a favorite place for picnicking, swimming, and fishing.

Soon after the Civil War, the notion went around among the locals, that money could be made from such a treasure. An inn and other buildings were built, and since so much was made of the medicinal powers of the cool pure water, the idea of a health resort arose.

A group of businessmen formed the Cartersburg Magnetic Springs Association, and bought the farm on which the springs lay, in the late 1800s. With their commercial promotion, the springs became increasingly popular. By 1906, all rooms in the hotel they had built were booked for the summer, and wealthy families, with their nannies to look after the children, crowded the resort. Unfortunately, in September of that year a

A group of visitors to the Magnetic Springs Hotel prepare for a game of croquet. The health resort, located near Cartersburg, enjoyed a period of prosperity in the late 1890s.

Guilford Township Historical Society Collection/Plainfield Public Library

fire started in the bathhouse, and spread along a wooden walkway to the hotel. While townspeople and visitors tried to save it, the hotel was lost and the resort was never rebuilt.

With several streams and creeks to power them, the county was once rich with mills, which supplied the flour, bran, wheat, and cornmeal for the residents.

One enterprising family, the Nicholsons, ran a steam-powered sorghum mill from the middle 1800s until 1955. The mill was located west and south of Danville, along what is now County Road 125W, which some people still call Sorghum Mill Road. Since sorghum thrives in the same growing conditions as corn, it was a staple on many farms. In the fall, families brought their sorghum canes by the wagon load, or later by trucks, and the Nicholson mill pressed out the juice and processed it into molasses. Thick sorghum molasses, poured from jugs carefully stored to last all year, was a favorite to sweeten an early morning

Hendricks County breakfast biscuit. During one year in World War II, Cyrus Nicholson made fifteen thousand gallons of sorghum.

Canneries sprang up in several Hendricks County towns, to capitalize on the abundant food crops local farmers could produce, particularly tomatoes and corn.

Many early businesses came and went, but one—started in 1812 in Washington County near Salem, Indiana, and moved in 1875 to Guilford township—has thrived. What is now known as C. M. Hobbs & Sons, Inc., has been one of the largest and most successful nursery businesses in the country. Progress and development, spreading from Indianapolis and Plainfield, have finally merged at each edge of the nursery's property. Now much of the acreage is slated to become a commercial development. However, the family intends to carry on the nursery business, even as buildings rise in the surrounding fields that used to grow trees and shrubs.

The Nicholson family operated a sorghum mill from the 1890s until 1955. The sweetener was especially in demand during World Wars I and II, when sugar was rationed.

Guilford Township Historical Society Collection/Plainfield Public Library

152

Four years before the Indiana Territory became a state, Quakers, Dr. Benjamin Albertson and William Hobbs, migrated from North Carolina along with some other families, and settled in Salem, Indiana. Dr. Albertson cultivated trees and plants, and his son Oliver developed the nursery into the largest in the state.

In 1875 Oliver Albertson moved to Bridgeport, Indiana. He, his son Emery, and his son-in-law C. M. Hobbs developed a four- hundred-acre nursery beside the National Road, on land sharing parts of Hendricks and Marion Counties. After Emery Albertson retired in 1907, C. M. Hobbs continued the business, and it has remained in the Hobbs family for three generations. The office building still incorporates what once was a toll gate for the old National Road.

One of the early businesses in Plainfield was a franchised "treatment center" for alcoholism, drug abuse, and tobacco use. The Keeley Institute opened its doors in

Photo courtesy of C. M. Hobbs and Sons Nurseries, Inc.

Top: This is one of the earliest photographs of the Albertson-Hobbs Nursery, believed to be circa 1890s. One of the buildings still in use today was the toll house for the National Road which passed by the entrance to the nursery business. The business began in Salem, Indiana, in 1812 and was moved here in 1875.

Bottom: This overview gives a glimpse of the size of the operation which once had 500 acres in Hendricks and Marion Counties, and 50 acres in Dansville, New York, and another 40 acres near Topeka, Kansas planted in fruit trees. In the early 1900s the operation was shipping and receiving 200 to 300 boxcars of trees and shrubs annually.

Industrial Souvenir of Hendricks County, State of Indiana

Right: The Keeley Institute was housed in a former hotel. The drug withdrawal program was part of a national chain of treatment centers.

Below: Drugs and instruments confiscated from the patients at the Plainfield Keeley Institute were arranged in an advertising photo, along with the visage of Dr. A. P. W. Bridges, the director of the Institute.

Guilford Township Historical Society Collection/Plainfield Public Library

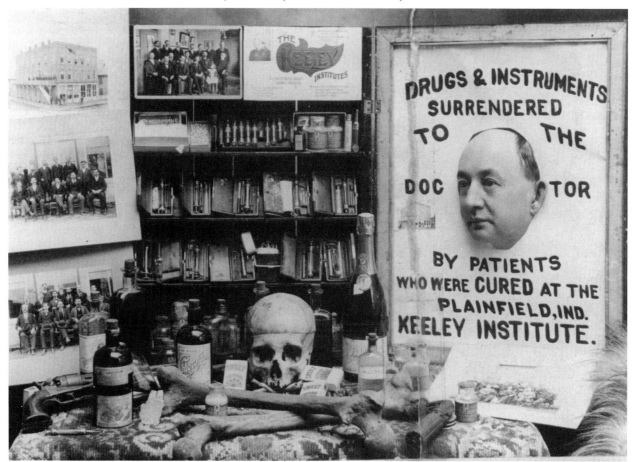

Guilford Township Historical Society Collection/Plainfield Public Library

1891, and supplied treatment until 1918, when the owners thought the enactment of Prohibition would make their business unnecessary. The cure was administered in a four-week program, in which, the first week the patient was injected with medicine, and in subsequent weeks, they took their medication by teaspoonfuls, every two hours. During the first three days, alcoholics were encouraged to drink as much liquor as they wished. By the third day, the medication reacted with the alcohol, and the patient became ill at the sight of an alcoholic drink. Drug addiction was treated the same way, but usually took longer. Tobacco use often was "cured" in a much shorter time.

The Institute hosted annual reunions of the "graduates," including many prominent citizens, judges, lawyers, artists, and a famous poet or two, who paid $100 for alcohol treatment, $25 a week for tobacco addiction, for as long as it took, and $25 per week for drug addiction for, an approxi-

mate, four to eight week cure. During its twenty-seven years in business, the Keeley Institute treated over four thousand patients, and claimed a 95 percent cure rate.

During the summers of old, Hendricks County residents and visitors would spend some leisure time, watching harness racing at the tracks, scattered across the county as horses' hooves thundered around the oval track. Now, in the warm months in the far eastern portion of Lincoln Township, another flat piece of ground vibrates with the throaty roar of powerful racing engines. Indianapolis Raceway Park opened for its first motorsport competition in 1960, with a National Hot Rod Association drag race. The IRP complex, located on U.S. 136, only a few miles from the Indianapolis Motor Speedway race course, was conceived, in 1958, by Tom Binford, Frank Dicke, and Roger Ward, as a place for a good half mile oval track. They then decided to include a 2.5 mile road race course, and almost as an

"Graduates" of the Keeley Institute returned for a reunion in 1900. The group was called the "Bichloride of Gold Club" after the compound used to treat addiction. The building was decorated with banners of blue and gold.

afterthought, included a drag strip. While world famous for the annual NHRA U.S. Nationals drag races, sponsored by the current owners of the track, the National Hot Rod Association, the track is busy 250 days a year, with events on the three race courses. With attendance of over a half million visitors during a season, Indianapolis Raceway Park is the third largest taxpayer in Hendricks County, and the largest in Lincoln Township, according to Jeff Dakin, director of operations in 1999.

Crowds gathered for the NHRA Nationals in 1979. Revenues from the Indianapolis Raceway Park make it the third largest taxpayer in Hendricks County.

Guilford Township Historical Society Collection/Plainfield Public Library

Guilford Township Historical Society Collection/Plainfield Public Library

Left: The village blacksmith shop was an important part of the rural community. N. M. Frazier advertised his ability to perform "work of all kinds" and added a lucky horseshoe over the door.

Below: The Edmonson brothers, Columbus and Charles were virtually business magnates of Clayton in the turn of the century. A large lumber company and farm implement and new buggy sales store—which carried McCormack harvesting machines, John Deere plows, Studebaker, and troy wagons, and fine buggies from Laporte and Wescott manufacturers—bore the Edmonson name.

Industrial Souvenir of Hendricks County, State of Indiana

Hendricks County Historical Society

Hendricks County Historical Society

Industrial Souvenir of Hendricks County, State of Indiana

st Side Public Square, Danville, Ind.

Hendricks County Historical Society

Top left: Home and business were connected in the minds of Hendricks County citizens during the nineteenth and early twentieth centuries. The home of the John T. Bell family in Pittsboro was literally connected to the family business. The retired county sheriff offered "CUT RATE FOR CASH" when he opened his store in the late 1890s.

Bottom left: In 1900, burgeoning Clayton built three new business blocks for its houses of commerce and the wealthy populace began to construct many elegant residences, complete with gracious lawns and wrought iron fences.

Top right: Business was booming at Danville in the early 1900s. The location of the county seat and the college made the town an attractive site for merchants. The east side of the square, pictured around 1910, contained more than a dozen businesses.

Bottom right: Many businesses commemorated their success with a photograph. In the late 1890s, Ira Martin (standing left) and Ray McDaniel posed outside their feed and fuel store in Coatesville with one of their delivery wagons.

Guilford Township Historical Society Collection/Plainfield Public Library

Top: This neat store operated for over forty years in North Salem according to Mrs. R. L. Proffitt. Note the National Biscuit Company cracker bins between the two customers on the left. This scene appears to be circa 1910s.

Bottom: The hardware store, such as the establishment of deAtley & Spangler at Lizton, carried necessary items for both farm and home, from harnesses to washing machines.

Industrial Souvenir of Hendricks County, State of Indiana

Guilford Township Historical Society Collection/Plainfield Public Library

Above: C. A. Edmonson's vehicle and implement store was located south of the railroad in Clayton.

Right: With the practice of the "dismal trade," in 1904, O. D. Nash (undertaker) had a second business of livery to sustain him during outbreaks of good health.

Hendricks County Historical Society

Right: Although they still made house calls, doctors at the turn of the century often had a small office building erected adjacent to their homes. The office of Dr. John L. Marsh at Brownsburg is a typical example. A hitching post was available for use of visiting patients.

Hendricks County Historical Society

Below: Wealthy patrons such as the Dr. Rileus Jones family shown here often brought the nanny to watch after the children as the adults relaxed at the popular Cartersburg Magnetic Springs Resort.

Guilford Township Historical Society Collection/Plainfield Public Library

Hendricks County Historical Society

Water from the Cartersburg Springs was hauled to Indianapolis and points beyond in this 1915 Mais truck driven by Jim McCamick.

Hendricks County Historical Society

A tuberculosis sanitarium called Rockwood was located in Washington Township in the early 1900s. It emphasized fresh air as a part of the treatment, and patients slept with open windows—even in winter. It had a high death rate. The development of vaccines for the disease hastened the demise of such sanitariums.

Hendricks County Historical Society

Hendricks County Historical Society

Industrial Souvenir of Hendricks County, State of Indiana

Like the district schools, most of the old interurban stations in the county have been converted to other uses. Pictured (**top left**) is the Brownsburg station circa the early 1900's. At the demise of the interurban the building was the location for many businesses, including this garden center (**bottom left**).

Top right: The press room of the Publishing Association of Friends produced all the publications for the Sunday Schools for the Friends in the U.S. and Canada beginning in 1901. They also produced commercial publications such as the Industrial Souvenir of Hendricks County, in 1904 from which many of the pictures in this book are taken.

Bottom right: The first appearance of the telephone in the county was as an experiment at Central Normal College in the late 1870s. By 1904, the Consolidated Telephone Company, headquartered at Danville, had twelve hundred subscribers who paid 3 and ⅓ cents per day for the service.

Industrial Souvenir of Hendricks County, State of Indiana

Guilford Township Historical Society Collection/Plainfield Public Library

10 Recreation

ALL WORK AND NO PLAY MAKES JACK a dull boy. That old phrase applied in early times in Hendricks County as well as now. The settlers of Hendricks County gathered for socializing whenever they could find the time from farming and running businesses, and music usually played some part.

While most of the early entertainment consisted of the occasional musician performing solo or with one or two friends, as the population grew music makers banded together. While seldom boasting formal uniforms, organized bands began playing in the 1870s on Saturday nights in Pittsboro, Danville, Plainfield, and other communities around the county. North Salem was especially known for musical groups such as the Ladies Choral Union and the North Salem Mandolin Orchestra.

Right: Music had charm among the citizens of Pittsboro, who formed a town band in the late 1800s.

Below: Musical talent often was a family trait. Members of the Shirley family formed a musical trio. Ettie, on the left, strummed the guitar, while brother Alva played the violin, with Fred accompanying on the banjo.

Guilford Township Historical Society Collection/Plainfield Public Library

Hendricks County Historical Society

Central Normal College in Danville and the Plainfield Central Academy both had orchestras. In the 1930s and 1940s, the Hoosier Symphony Orchestra and Choral, organized by two professors at Central Normal, regularly entertained the community and performed for the school's opera guild.

There were two songs of note written in Hendricks County.

An instructor at the Plainfield Boy's School, Thomas P. Westendorf, penned a song in 1876 that still melts the hearts of Irishmen everywhere, although he was not Irish. "I'll Take You Home Again, Kathleen," became extremely popular and can be heard in Irish pubs today.

Ned Clay of the North Salem Boys Band penned "Indianapolis, We Love you," with lyrics by Raymond Trulock in 1925. It was played when Lew Shank, as mayor of Indianapolis, hosted a Mardi Gras-like celebration. It was adopted as the official Hoosier Capital Song, according to a hand written note on a copy of the sheet music at the Indianapolis Public Library.

In the very early days, a group's "pitching in" to help one another would often be turned into a festive occasion. One such event, called a "log rolling," would take place whenever a land owner needed to clear a piece of land of the thick tree stands.

Old newspapers give accounts of the many parades held in the communities, which always brought a turnout of onlookers as participants celebrated a national holiday, or a local event.

Some of the liveliest times were enjoyed when traveling orators spoke on the courthouse square or in a local park. James Whitcomb Riley, the famous Greenfield poet is known to have given readings of his poetry in Danville before a packed audience.

Traveling stock companies of players would arrive in town and entertain the pop-ulace with performances of classic works or the latest play from the east.

People living in the late 1800s and early 1900s looked forward to the week-long Chautauqua which would arrive by train during the summer months and set up large tents in a park or in the school yard. In the mornings, the children of the town would be entertained by magicians and puppet shows, while in the afternoon, a lecturer or soloist would perform. Evening entertainment would often be the "headliner" act, a play, or a concert.

Excerpt from an article, by the author, Linda Balough, appearing in the "Hendricks County Flyer," August of 1997.

On June 2, 1877, at the elegant farm of Dr. Allen Furnas, south of Danville near "Sorghum Mill Church," an event of great magnitude took place. The governor of the state of Indiana, Gov. James "Blue Jeans" Williams joined the good doctor in conducting a "log roll" which was the center of attention of some 2,000 or more citizens and a multitude from the press. Buggies, wagons, and saddle horses clustered around the showplace home as the spectators and participants, dressed in their finery, gathered for the spectacle. All the men wore white shirts with starched or paper col-lars, except the governor, who wore his customary suit of blue jean material and a white linen vest, and the doctor, who wore overalls. The ladies were arrayed in their finest dresses. According to the *Indianapolis Herald*, when the crowd cheered as the governor arrived, he "showed his appreciation by turning a somersault and alighting on his heels, which he then raised high in the air and cracked together with a loud and firm cock-a-doodle-doo."

Furnas and Williams were both in the Indiana state legislature and, while members of opposing parties, became friends. They often disagreed on the proper method of clearing wooded land, however, and challenged each other to a contest the next time one needed a "log

Everyone loves a parade. This was the Centennial Celebration Parade in Danville in 1924. Hendricks County officially came into being on April 1, 1824. Notice the brick pavement here at the corner of Main and Jefferson.

Hendricks County Historical Society

roll" accomplished. When Furnas decided the 10 acres at the corner of the roads should be cleared, Williams had been recently elected to office. Both parties must have determined the event to be a political coup and the press was notified and the party (held without whiskey, profanity, fights, or betting, according to the *Danville Union*) was on. (The refreshments, the *Herald* told, were buttermilk, and "swankey" a mixture of vinegar, molasses, and water.)

Hendricks County Historical Society

A log rolling on the Furnas farm became the subject of an engraving entitled "Governor Williams as a Farmer." The governor, who was nicknamed "Blue Jeans" for his apparel, is standing to the right of the oxen. His resemblance to Abraham Lincoln was noted in his political campaigns. The governor's host, Dr. Allen Furnas, is the hatless man to the governor's right.

One Danville resident first appeared with P. T. Barnum's Circus, operated his own traveling circus, and for a time, operated an unsuccessful candy store and pool hall in his home town.

John Hanson Craig was born in Iowa in 1847, and weighed 11 pounds. Before he was a year old, he weighed 77 pounds. As a two-year old, Johnnie Craig won the $1,000 prize at P. T. Barnum's Baby Show in New York as the world's heaviest baby—he weighed in at 206 pounds!

Craig began traveling with Barnum's Circus as a teen tipping the scales at somewhere around 500 pounds. The Circus's 700 pound fat lady, Mary Jane Kesler, was from Hendricks County, and in 1869 John Craig and Mary Kesler married and started their own traveling show. When not on the road, they lived in a lit-

tle blue house on North Washington Street in Danville.

John Craig—or as he was known in show business, Powers—at an adult weight of 907 pounds, presented a formidable task for local tailor, Harry McPhetridge. Craig stood 6 feet 5 inches tall, measured 8 feet 4 inches around the hips, and 65 inches around his chest and required nearly twenty-seven yards of cloth to build a suit of clothes. After completing one of Craig's suits, McPhetridge displayed it in the window, from which three men "borrowed" the coat and, buttoning it around all three, marched around the square.

After his first wife died, and was buried in Mt. Pleasant Cemetery in Hendricks County, Craig married another showperson from Tippecanoe County, Indiana,

"Broadsides" were large sheets of paper with advertising for various types of traveling entertainment companies. Members of the troupe would arrive several weeks ahead of the company and pay local children to "plaster" the broadsides around the town. Two Amo boys posed proudly alongside an advertisement for an upcoming Hippodrome Show at Danville in 1900.

Hendricks County Historical Society

Jennie Ryan. She was a petite, dark-haired woman who performed with a boa constrictor. They had a child, Helen, in 1890, and thereafter toured together.

An April 21, 1892 issue of the Hendricks *County Republican*, announces the pending appearance of "Craig's Congress of Wonders," and states, "He proposes to give a refined entertainment with nothing to mar the feelings of the most fastidious. Ladies and children can attend without an escort."

The Craigs divorced twice, and Jennie left the child with John and returned home to Tippecanoe County.

When John died in 1894, a custom-made coffin was constructed: 6 feet 9 inches in length, 34 inches wide and 30 inches deep. As had been necessary for his first wife's funeral, the window casing had to be removed to bring out Craig's coffin to the waiting wagon. He, too, was buried in Mt. Pleasant Cemetery.

Six months later, Jennie returned for Helen and to settle the estate and married William Roddy, Craig's manager, and the person who had been caring for the child.

Hendricks County Historical Society

John Hanson Craig, "the heaviest man alive," made his home in Danville when he was not touring with his circus and sideshow.

Generated by advance postings of colorful advertising posters and hand bills, the excitement ran rampant when circuses occasionally rolled into town. Children and adults alike eagerly attended, in awe of the lions, tigers, and acrobats.

A novel entertainment, the "magic lantern" show began appearing in some meeting houses, where the room was darkened and an image was cast on a wall or screen by shining a lamp behind a glass plate. Not long after, came the "moving picture show."

Coatesville residents get comfortable before viewing an outdoor motion picture. The movie-goers brought their own seating for the show.

Hendricks County Historical Society

Guilford Township Historical Society Collection/Plainfield Public Library

Horse races were not always confined to the county's racetracks; this one in very early Coatesville drew a sizable crowd. Notice the ladies chose to watch from the protection of the porches.

In Coatesville, with the advent of the movies, the town closed the main street and hung a screen across the road. The surrounding population brought their chairs, gathered in the street and enjoyed an evening's entertainment as the night's feature was projected onto the portable screen.

Soon, movie theater houses sprang up in nearly all of the larger towns. A trip to the movies became a regular weekend pastime, and presented stiff competition to live plays in high school auditoriums and churches.

Sports became big attractions, and the harness horse racing at the County Fairgrounds track near where the Danville High School is now, and one at Franklin and Green Streets in Brownsburg, brought people from Indianapolis and surrounding counties to watch the competition at the turn of the century. Some races were even staged in the streets of town. Horse shows were held all around the county in the summer and competition for the title "Best of Show" was fierce.

Baseball, the National Game, grew in popularity during the years after the Civil War. Most towns had a number of "town teams" who played against each other for recreation and entertainment. Danville had the largest number of teams, including two "ladiesí teams," the Daisies and the Darlings. The Danville Browns, pictured around 1914, participated in amateur leagues from the 1880s until the 1930s.

Hendricks County Historical Society

After the Civil War, the king of sports was baseball. Nearly every town had at least one team. In Danville, there were the Reds, Cyclones, Sluggers, Choctaws, Comets, West Main Street Cool Heads, the Paralyzers, and the Browns. A carpenter named "Big Sam" Thompson who played for the Browns went on to hold baseball world records and find a place in the Baseball Hall of Fame.

Big Sam was a powerful slugger and still holds the record for RBIs (runs batted in) with an average of .921 per game. His record of 127 career home runs was finally topped by Babe Ruth, twenty-four years after Thompson had retired from the game to be a U.S. Marshall in Detroit.

Samuel Luther Thompson was born in Danville in 1860, as one of six boys who according to Danville reporter Lannes McPhetridge, "Were a band of

boys wandering with loose reins in the highways and woodland in and around Danville . . . They were the first to go barefoot in the spring and the last to put on shoes in autumn."

One day, in 1884, while twenty-three-year-old Sam was playing ball, a scout from Evansville came to look at an older brother, Cy. When the scout found out Cy (who everyone said was the better player) was over twenty-six, he turned his attention to the 6'2", 210 pound younger brother, and finally convinced Sam to try professional baseball for the Evansville team. He played there, went to Indianapolis, and then was recruited by Detroit, where in 1887, he helped win the World Championship trophy. According to the *Detroit Times*, Sam went from ". . . at the age of 23, discovering he could play ball—and within three years becoming one of the

continued overleaf

greatest batters the game ever produced."

In a time when baseball players were considered to be combative, arrogant ruffians, Sam stood out as a man of character. The *Chicago News*, in 1887, says, "Men everywhere are proud of him because he so splendidly illustrates well-applied virility, and the women all adore him because there is combined with his superb athletic qualities, a modesty that is inexpressibly charming."

At his death, years after he had retired from the game, newspapers reported a huge crowd of people, including million-aires and federal judges, overflowing in the yard of his little cottage home.

It may have been Thompson's quiet demeanor and lack of notoriety that delayed his placement in the Hall of Fame until 1974, the same year Mickey Mantle and Whitey Ford were inducted.

Samuel Luther Thompson, known as "Big Sam," was a natural talent when it came to the National Sport. The Danville native was elected to the Baseball Hall of Fame at Cooperstown, New York. A ball diamond at Ellis Park has been named in his honor.

Baseball Hall of Fame Library, Cooperstown, N.Y.

Other team sports, such as football and basketball became popular, and Hendricks County residents, like other Hoosiers, filled the high school gymnasiums and the bleachers at the football fields to cheer their teams to victory.

Other entertainment centered around the county's agricultural prowess. The County Fair was begun in 1853 and held until the grounds were sold in 1880. Even in years with no county fair, contests and livestock shows continued. Nearly everything grown on the farm could compete for a blue ribbon. The first Corn Contest was held in 1906. In school young people were taught how to raise and judge the best corn, hogs, sheep, and other farm production, so when the time came for the contests, competition was fierce. In about 1927 the fair was reestablished, and first, held on the square in Danville, later moved to where the South Elementary School is now, and then to the grounds of the county garage. The current Hendricks County Fairgrounds and 4-H Center on Old U.S. 36, or Main Street in Danville, were set up within the County Farm acreage in 1956 and enjoy a ninety-nine-year lease.

The local horse show was a time to exhibit the finest in horseflesh as well as the fanciest carts and surreys. Owners and breeders examined the stock to find the best combinations to produce "next year's models."

Hendricks County Historical Society

177

Hendricks County Historical Society

Top: The smallest town could boast its own orchestra. Amo, in Clay Township, was no exception. Members of the band in 1905 included (left to right): Verlie Moon and Ozro Hadley, violins; Fred Shirley, bass violin; Verlie Rudd, violin; George Tincher, flute; Josephine Doty, piano; Lou Dill, drums; Ressie Hendricks, triangle; Alva Shirley, cornet; and Roy Nichols, clarion.

Bottom: Every town that could carry a tune had a band. Clayton's band posed with their instruments.

Guilford Township Historical Society Collection/Plainfield Public Library

The trotting competition was the gentleman's form of horse racing. The trotting park located at the west edge of Danville was formerly the site of the county fair. It included an oval track, grandstands for the spectators, and stables for the horses. An advertisement for the park appeared in the September 4, 1884 issue of the Hendricks County *Republican*.

Hendricks County Historical Society

Kids loved playing in
1906 just as well as today.
However, when little sister
wanted the boys to be
on her "team" this may
not have been what they
had in mind.

Hendricks County Historical Society

Left: The latest in football gear was modeled by an unidentified player in the photography studio of O. P. Phillips of Clay Township circa 1900. Safety features included shin guards, padded knickers, a padded leather helmet (hanging from belt), and a hard leather nose guard (hanging around neck).

Bottom: Riding (albeit sidesaddle) was an acceptable form of recreation for the young ladies in the early 1900s.

Hendricks County Historical Society

Guilford Township Historical Society Collection/Plainfield Public Library

Clayton's Jolly Belles were a fun loving group of young ladies who went to school together in the 1900s. They had several photographs made of their antics wearing their creative costumes.

184

Bibliography

"Conspicuous leisure" was indicated by the swing glider, a popular piece of outdoor furniture in the early 1900s. A couple in Amo could take time from their busy day to relax under the shade in their front yard.

Carlisle, James C. *A Simple and Vital Design: The Story of the Indiana Post Office Murals.* Indianapolis: Indiana Historical Society, 1995.

Frazier, Charles. *Cold Mountain.* New York: Atlantic Monthly Press, 1997.

Greenapple, H. R., ed. *D. C. Stevenson Irvington 0492: The Demise of the Grand Dragon of the Indiana Ku Klux Klan.* Plainfield, Ind.: SGS Publications, Inc., 1989.

Hadley, Hon. John V., ed. *History of Hendricks County Indiana: Her People, Industries and Institutions.* Indianapolis: B. F. Bowen & Co., Inc., 1914.

Hadley, John V. *Seven Months A Prisoner.* 1898. Reprint, with an introduction by Libbe K. Hughes. Hanover, Indiana: The Nugget Publishers, 1998.

History of Hendricks County Indiana. Chicago: Interstate Publishing Company, 1885.

Kennedy, Peg, and Frankie Konvsek. *Village of Brownsburg.* Robinson, Illinois: Lamplight Publishing, 1998.

McCord, Shirley S., compiled by. *Travel Accounts of Indiana 1679–1961.* Indiana Historical Collections, Vol. XLVII. Indianapolis: Indiana Historical Bureau, 1970.

McDowell, John, ed. *The History of Hendricks County 1914–1976.* Danville, Ind.: The Hendricks County Historical Society, 1976.

Post, Margaret Moore. *Our Town Yesterday, Plainfield, Indiana, a Pictorial History.* Plainfield, Ind.: Joe Lease Publisher, 1974.

Pritchard, Ruth Mitchell. *Honoring Our Heritage in Indiana.* Plainfield, Ind.: Mill Creek School Corporation, for the Indiana Sesquicentennial Committee, 1974.

Raidabaugh, Walter, ed. *Industrial Souvenir of Hendricks County, State of Indiana.* Plainfield, Indiana: Friends Press, 1904.

The Indiana Historian. Indianapolis, Indiana: Indiana Historical Bureau, State of Indiana, August 1994, periodical.

The Islamic Society of North America. *The Islamic Center.* Plainfield, Ind.: The Islamic Society of North America, n.d., pamphlet.

Index

About the Authors

Linda Balough (left) and Betty Bartley.

Linda Balough was born in Owensboro, Kentucky. She lived for a time in western New York, and in Hancock and Marion Counties in Indiana before settling in Hendricks County in 1974 with her husband, Timothy.

She worked in a wide variety of fields including sales, management, and real estate and worked for the U.S. government for a number of years. She was a rural mail carrier at the Plainfield Post Office for seventeen years, and carried the mail in the Avon and Plainfield areas.

Balough is a member of the Hendricks County Historical Society and the Indiana Historical Society, and has been active in several civic organizations.

She is now a full time freelance writer. Balough has contributed to the Hendricks County Flyer and currently, to the *Indianapolis Star* and *Indianapolis News* as well as a number of other local and national publications, and produces the newsletter and press releases for the Plainfield Community School Corporation. This is her first book, and she is currently conducting research for a Civil War historical novel.

Betty Bartley has been a life-long resident of Hendricks County. Her maternal relatives were among the early settlers of the county in the 1830s.

She resides on the farm purchased by her parents in the mid-1950s. Her father operated a dairy farm there for nearly thirty years. A few years after his death, she returned the farm to the dairy business and continues his interest in raising Holstein cattle.

She has worked in the local history divisions of the Plainfield and Danville Public Libraries. She is currently president of the Hendricks County Historical Society and curator of the Hendricks County Museum.

Ms. Bartley is a member of the Indiana Historical Society, the American Association for State and Local History, the Association for Gravestone Studies, and the Civil War Roundtable of West Central Indiana.

She is the current editor of the *Hendricks County History Bulletin* and *The Chronicler* (published by the Hendricks County Historical Society). She has also written articles on local history for *The Republican* newspaper.